SAVING SEEDS

The Gardener's Guide to Growing and Storing Vegetable and Flower Seeds

Marc Rogers

Illustrations by Polly Alexander

STOREY BOOKS
Schoolhouse Road
Pownal, Vermont 05261

*The mission of Storey Communications is to serve our customers
by publishing practical information that encourages personal independence
in harmony with the environment.*

Cover design by Carol Jessop
Text design by Judy Eliason
Illustrations by Polly Alexander
Edited by Paul Howes and Ben Watson

Portions of this book were originally published by Garden Way Publishing in 1978 as *Growing & Saving Vegetable Seeds*.

Storey Books are available for special premium and promotional uses and for customized editions. For further information, please call Storey's Custom Publishing Department at 1-800-793-9396.

Printed in the United States by Courier
20 19 18

Library of Congress Cataloging-in-Publication Data

Rogers, Marc.
    Saving Seeds : the gardener's guide to growing and storing vegetable and flower seeds / Marc Rogers ; illustrations by Polly Alexander
        p.   cm.
    "A down-to-earth gardening book".
    Includes bibliographical references.
    ISBN 0-88266-634-7 (pbk.)
    1. Vegetables — Seeds. 2. Flowers — Seeds. 3. Vegetables — Seeds — Storage. 4. Flowers — Seeds — Storage. 5. Vegetable gardening. 6. Flower gardening. I. Title.
SB324.75.R633 1990
635.0421—dc20
                                                                        90-50353
                                                                        CIP

Contents

Dicotyledoneae

PART III: THE FLOWERS

The Best Flowering Ornamentals to Save for Seed

PART I
BASIC INFORMATION

CHAPTER 1

Why Raise Seeds?

A sneeze several years ago started me along the circuitous route toward growing seeds to save.

I had heard the arguments against growing seeds for so long that I began believing them all. Don't grow seeds, the garden books say. These various arguments all seem to boil down to one main point: that you and I really aren't smart enough to save seeds. Our grandparents did, as did their parents; as did countless generations reaching almost back to our ancestors who first swung out of a tree, but the plain truth is that the human line has petered out a bit, and that you and I aren't capable of growing our own seeds.

Then comes the final point, the real clincher: Seeds are cheap.

I won't argue that seeds at almost any price are a bargain. Think for a moment of someone building a kit that would include all of the parts and the directions for building a celery plant. Think of being able to do this, then offering it so that the entire package — parts, directions, and container — weighs but $1/70,000$ of an ounce.

Nature has designed such a kit — a celery seed.

But *are* seeds really cheap? I hadn't thought of it too much, only realizing that each January my seed bill grew larger and larger, while my garden stayed the same. And noticing that I now paid $2 for what I thought was a dollar's worth of peas.

Then came that sneeze. Surprising how it snuck up on me. Surprising how loud it was. Surprising me so that my right hand snapped skyward. My right hand at that moment was holding a few seeds — $5 worth of tiny petunia seeds. The dustlike seeds shot up, then were caught in the gale of the sneeze and scattered to, in this case, the one wind.

The seeds were gone, but not forgotten. For that incident started me thinking more about seed costs. My handy calculator soon told me that, if I had managed to sneeze away a pound of those petunia seeds, instead of $1/128$ of an ounce, my sneeze bill for the day would have amounted to more than $10,000. That's much more than gold costs, and it certainly shows that seeds aren't cheap.

I noticed, too, that seed packets were changing. Only infrequently did they tell me the number of seeds to be found therein. The price for a packet most often was more than a dollar. And no longer were the packets fat with seed. Some were downright slim, even undernourished, in shape.

Today's prices haven't dropped from those of several years ago when I first began to watch them. The move of prices has been in the opposite direction. A good hybrid tomato seed sells for $5 for $1/32$ of an ounce. I'll save you the calculating and tell you it's $2,560 a pound — and the seed is even more expensive if you buy it by the packet instead of in the comparatively large increment of $1/32$ of an ounce.

Clearly, I had found one good reason for raising and saving

seeds. To save money. The day of the nickel packet of seeds was over. It was time I looked for another, almost-free source of seeds.

Then I began to wonder if there might be other good reasons for growing and saving seeds.

I immediately thought of a Lebanese family in town. Their grandparents had arrived on Ellis Island years ago, bringing with them very little money, only a few clothes, a handful of squash seeds, and a headful of recipes for cooking those squash in the most delectable manner. Various grandchildren now are growing what must be the sixtieth generation of those seeds in this country, never giving this squash an opportunity to indulge its promiscuous habit of crossing with any other member of its not-so-immediate family.

Here was another reason for growing and saving seed. To preserve and perpetuate varieties that could die out. Look at a seed catalog of ten or twenty years ago, and compare the varieties of seeds found there with current offerings. Many have been dropped, some for good reason, others because it doesn't pay to carry too many varieties. Perhaps one of those dropped was exactly what you wanted, because of its taste or keeping qualities or looks. If you had saved this seed, you could have continued a variety now forgotten. Your choice of which varieties to grow would not be entirely in the hands of the seed companies.

Many good old heirloom strains, no longer offered commercially, have already been lost. Some of the vegetables we enjoy today — the Royalty bean and Clemson Spineless okra for example — are still available to us because one family nurtured and handed down the seed for generations. Once a variety dies out, it cannot be retrieved.

If you have seed of a special, obscure, unusual, or heirloom vegetable variety, you — and many other people — might someday be glad that you kept the strain vital by planting and saving it.

If you raise and save seed, you are producing seed for *your* garden, and, by careful selection over several generations of plants, you can produce plants best suited to *your* climate and *your* gardening conditions. No one else but you can do this. Flavor, pest and disease resistance, early bearing, and size are among the many characteristics that can be enhanced by judicious selection over a period of years.

Years ago seeds became scarce as the number of home gardeners spurted. Something like this could happen again in the future, caused by a truck strike, blizzard, postal mix-up, or failure of crops. If you have raised and saved seeds, such an event will not hamper your gardening activities one bit. In fact, if you have raised more seeds than you need, as most of us do, you will be able to help your neighbors in a most meaningful way.

If you have a keen eye as you observe, evaluate, select, and compare your plants, you may even discover something new and valuable. The chances may be against it, but good new strains of plants have been found and are being found, some by plant breeders and a few by observant everyday gardeners. One such person was a turn-of-the-century seed grower, Calvin N. Keeney of Leroy, New York, who is credited with originating nine new varieties of bean, among them the Burpee's Stringless Green Pod, still listed in the Burpee catalog and credited as having the "finest flavor."

There's one benefit on which you yourself will have to put a value; I can't. Let's say you first attempt something easy — saving peas. The year that you plant those peas, you will put them in the ground with a little extra care. They'll get the choice compost for encouragement. You'll spend a minute or two longer with them each time you cultivate around them. And, sure enough, they'll taste a bit sweeter than any other peas you raise that year. There'll be a deeper satisfaction in growing them. What's that worth to you?

The final reason for raising seed? To prove to those writers of gardening books that the human strain hasn't weakened to the point where it is incapable of growing vegetable seeds. Grandpa was a smart old codger, but not that smart. Maybe he just grew seeds for saving because no one told him he couldn't.

A Satisfying Hobby

Seed-growing can be a satisfying, fascinating hobby, and you can select your own level of involvement. Perhaps that will be at the easy level of growing your own peas and beans for seeds. Perhaps you'll try selecting your best carrots to replant the following spring or maintaining your own especially vibrant strain of marigold or zinnia. Perhaps you'll find a way to grow cauliflower seed without the use of a greenhouse (and write to tell me how to do it). Be assured, though, that you won't outgrow this hobby, no matter how much you experiment, no matter how much you learn.

If you have any doubts about this, look at some of our nation's historic figures — Thomas Jefferson is a good example — who found a lifetime of satisfaction from experimenting in this area. Or look at what some of today's professionals in the field are attempting. A single example is the present effort to give other plants the ability that many legumes have, to host soil organisms that change the nitrogen in the air to a form that can be used by the plant.

Obtaining and Exchanging Seeds

Obtaining seeds of some little-grown yet desirable vegetable and flower seeds is becoming a challenge. As seed companies merge, many marginally profitable seed lines are dropped, and commercial availability becomes restricted or ceases altogether. Fortunately, various seed-saving organizations have sprouted to perpetuate heirloom and other seldom-seen varieties.

The Seed Savers Exchange (Rural Route 3, Box 239, Decorah, Iowa 52101) is a nonprofit organization dedicated to "passing on our vegetable heritage." The exchange publishes information regarding seed saving and an annual list of varieties available through the membership. If you send a long self-addressed, stamped envelope, you will receive an informational pamphlet. The headquarters of a flower and herb exchange is located at the same address. Your county Cooperative Extension agent may also know of other local and regional seed exchanges in your area.

Keep in mind that quality control by amateur seed savers will vary greatly, and that there is no guarantee regarding fitness of seed obtained through exchanges.

The Andersen Horticultural Library's *Source List of Plants and Seeds* by Richard T. Isaacson and published by the University of Minnesota lists over 20,000 varieties of plants commercially available in North America. The list includes, for instance, 144 varieties of petunia and 140 varieties of bean. Many of the varieties are available only from a single source. Another excellent resource for varieties of vegetables is the *Garden Seed Inventory* published by the Seed Savers Exchange and available for $17.50, postage paid.

If there is a little-known variety you would like to grow, track it down and learn to save its seed before it becomes unavailable. You may wish to make seed that you save yourself available through an exchange. It is a satisfying way to help perpetuate our invaluable plant resources.

Arguments Against Growing Seeds

You will face discouraging arguments about raising seeds both in what you read and in your conversations with other gardeners. Arguments such as these:

You can't save the seeds of hybrids, because they won't produce true in the next generation. True, but there are many open-pollinated varieties that were growing successfully long before the hybrids were developed. This is not an attempt to belittle the contribution of hybrids. Most of them are more vigorous and produce more food or flowers per plant than do the open-pollinated varieties. But this doesn't mean that you can't find hardiness, top flavor, and great satisfaction in the varieties that you can raise for seed.

It is difficult for the gardener to isolate varieties and strains to avoid unwanted cross-pollination. And this is one of the reasons why the commercial seed-growing industry has moved westward into dry areas where there are fewer wild or garden varieties that may cross with the crop being grown for seed. Cross-pollination can be a major problem if the gardener works in the midst of other gardens where one has no control over what is being grown nearby. This at best is a delightful challenge to the gardener, and at worst may limit the breadth of seed-growing activities.

It is difficult in some areas to raise healthy seed because of the prevalence of certain diseases that carry-over on or in the seed. Not all species have seed-borne diseases. Careful *roguing* (or weeding-out) of unhealthy plants minimizes disease problems. Post-harvest measures can be taken in severe cases.

You are legally prohibited from saving seed from patented varieties. The Plant Variety Protection Act specifically allows the "farmer" to save seed for his own use and even to sell it to other "farmers." The U.S. Patent Office (separate from the Plant Variety Protection Office) is granting regular 17-year patents on certain seed-propagated plants from which one cannot legally save any seed for propagating purposes. Packets of these seeds should be clearly marked to indicate this patent protection.

Unwanted cross-pollination and faulty selection of seed plants results in the gradual deterioration or "running-out" of the seed. If and when it does, simply buy fresh seed to renew your stock.

Raising and saving seeds is not for everyone. The gardener whose only aim is to grow as much food as possible may not be interested. The gardener to whom the height of adventure is trying a new variety of tomato may back away. But the gardener who enjoys a challenge, who likes to try something different, who wonders about the "why" of the plant world — this person should try raising seeds. There will be failures and problems and disappointments, but these will only make the successes sweeter. And any small measure of self-reliance we can recapture in our overly dependent society is cause for satisfaction.

CHAPTER 2

What Is a Seed?

A seed is more, much more, than it appears to be. The hard, dry, distinctively shaped particles that we plant in our gardens are really dormant embryos — tiny, already formed plants encased in a protective coating. While we may think of seeds as a beginning, they are really links between generations of plants, vehicles for both the survival of the plant species and the spread of new life.

This one-chapter course in botany, while ignoring many fine points, exceptions, and variations, will give you the general idea of the process by which a seed is formed. This is necessary for a clear understanding of what you hope to accomplish when you save seed from your garden plants.

The well-timed miracle of the seed. First, the seed is planted. Next it thrusts down its root tip and unfolds its rudimentary leaves. Then those leaves reach above the soil as the roots expand. Finally, the tiny plant produces its first true leaves.

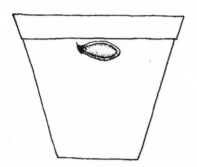 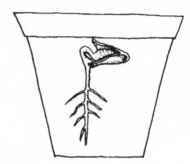

The Parts of a Seed

Difficult as it may be, imagine all the essential rudiments of a plant — leaves, stem, and root — encapsulated in a tiny, uniform parcel of life. That is indeed what each seed contains. Take the seed of a snap bean, for example. Soak the seed in water for a few hours and slip off the hard outer seed coat. It is easier to see, in the large seed of the bean, what is true of all seeds. There, compressed within that hard outer coating, are a set of rudimentary leaves called *cotyledons,* a bud that appears as a tiny tuft of leaves, a stem from which both cotyledons and bud arise, and — on the opposite end of the stem — a root tip.

Every seed has within it a reserve supply of carbohydrates, fat, protein, and minerals to nourish the dormant encapsulated plant. Some seeds, like the snap bean, lima bean, watermelon, and pumpkin, have thick, fleshy cotyledons (first leaves), which store nourishment. In other kinds of seeds, the young plant's food supply is found, not in the leaves, but in the *endosperm,* a material that oc-

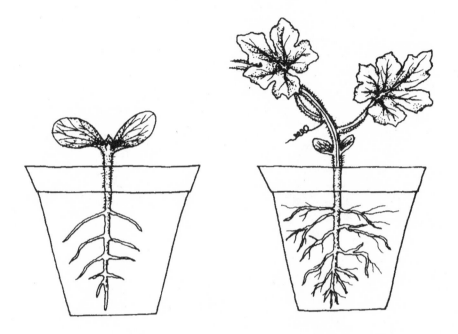

cupies the remaining space within the seed coat, beside and around the embryonic plant. The endosperm is floury in some kinds of plants; in others it is oily, waxy, or hard. Buckwheat and most cereal seeds, for example, contain a floury endosperm.

Far from being lifeless, seeds are actually living, resting plants in an embryonic state. Although the life processes of the seed are operating at a very low ebb, they are operating. Seeds carry on internal metabolic activity while they are dormant. They absorb moisture from the air. The stored food of the endosperm or the cotyledons combines with that moisture to form a soluble, and therefore usable, form of plant food for the resting embryo.

Kinds of Seeds

Although there is a great variety of size, shape, texture, and hardness in the seeds that flowering plants produce, most embryonic plants

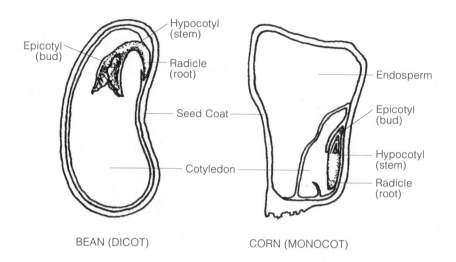

Epicotyl (bud)

Hypocotyl (stem)

Radicle (root)

Endosperm

Epicotyl (bud)

Hypocotyl (stem)

Radicle (root)

Seed Coat

Cotyledon

BEAN (DICOT)

CORN (MONOCOT)

A seed and its many parts.

(seeds) follow the same general design. They have two primary leaves with root tip and stem and sometimes with endosperm enclosed in a protective covering. Plants that have two cotyledons — the largest group of seed-bearing plants — are called *dicots.*

A smaller group, termed *monocots,* produces seed containing only one cotyledon. As you've probably noticed, the large family of grasses, to which corn, rye, and other grains belong, sends up a single shoot when the seed germinates, rather than the paired leaves that form on most other vegetable crops. Onions, too, belong to this group.

While some seeds will germinate at any time, there are many others that follow an internal time clock, a rhythm that insures (as much as is possible) that when the seed does germinate, conditions will be right for its growth. Some seeds must undergo cold or freezing temperatures in order to break dormancy. Still others need light to germinate. Lettuce seed may refuse to germinate in hot weather, when chances for the success of the plant are lower than in cool seasons.

If you remember only one fact from this quick crash course in botany, let it be this: Seeds are alive.

CHAPTER 3

How Seeds Are Formed

More than half the plants that grow on our earth are flowering plants. Many of the flowers are small and inconspicuous, like those of wheat and corn, but the seeds they produce have made possible some of the most influential plant improvements that people have been able to work out.

A flower's purpose in life is to produce seed. Although flowers differ tremendously in color, size, and complexity, each is uniquely equipped to form seed. Two parts of the blossom are essential to seed production: the *stamen,* or pollen-bearing part of the plant, and the *pistil,* which receives the pollen and nurtures the future seeds. The long, thin stalk of the stamen is called the *filament.* The pollen

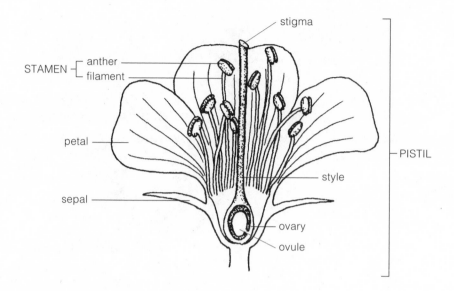

The parts of a flower.

sacs on the ends of the filaments are *anthers*. The stamen, with its filaments and anthers, is sometimes called the "male" part of the plant. The pistil, or "female" part, includes the *stigma*, or pollen-receptive region, the style, a long, thin tube leading from the stigma to the ovary, and the *ovary* itself, a cavity containing one or more *ovules* (eggs).

Seed is formed from the union of a ripe ovule and a grain of fertilizing pollen. When a pollen grain lands on the stigma of a receptive species, perhaps carried there by the wind or a bee, it begins to grow, putting forth a long thread of living matter that grows down through the style, enters the ovary, and penetrates an ovule, where it enters the embryo sac. The two cells — that of the pollen and that of the "egg" — unite to form a single living cell, called a *zygote*, which then has the power to multiply. This single-celled zygote — much divided and enlarged and finally matured — becomes the embryo of the new plant, that rudimentary leaf-bud-stem-root that is somehow all there in even the tiniest of seeds. The ovule exterior develops into the *seed coat.*

And what about the *endosperm,* that layer of nourishment for the new plant? How is it formed? There's an answer for that question, too; at least, botanists know what the process involves. (The why of the intricate impulses that cause these things to happen remains a mystery.) Although the grain of pollen, when first formed, was a single cell, it has usually split to form two cells by the time it reaches the stigma. One of these cells, you will remember, unites with the embryo sac of the ovule to form the zygote, which will grow into an embryonic plant. The second cell joins with other minute parts of the embryo sac — called *nuclei* — to form the endosperm, after much division and redivision of cells.

The ovary, usually containing multiple seeds, develops into the fruit, which we sometimes call a vegetable, and which is often the end product of our gardening efforts. Examples are tomatoes and peppers.

Once the embryonic plant within the seed has formed completely, growth stops and the seed enters a period of dormancy during which, as mentioned earlier, the plant consumes minute amounts of energy from the stored endosperm, just enough to keep it on "hold." The seed is alive, barely, but it should grow or develop no further until it is planted.

CHAPTER 4

Annuals, Biennials, and Perennials

Annuals

Let's start with the easiest to grow, the annuals, those garden plants that can be grown from seed to maturity and then allowed to go to seed themselves, all within the span of one growing season.

Some plants that are grown as annuals in the average North American garden, such as tomatoes, peppers, and lima beans, are actually perennials in their native tropics.

Other annuals, such as spinach, lettuce, wheat, and some rye plants, may survive a mild winter after fall planting and produce seed in the spring as if they were biennials. Hardy annuals will produce more seed in mild-winter areas when planted in the fall and carried through the winter than when matured in extremely hot summer weather.

With these exceptions, annuals will bear seed the same year they are planted. They need no special pampering, only to be given their normal cultural requirements and to be planted early enough in the season to give them time to ripen seed before they are killed by frost.

The common vegetables that are annuals include bean, broccoli, Chinese cabbage, corn, cucumber, eggplant, lettuce, muskmelon, pea, pepper, pumpkin, most radishes, spinach, and squash. Annual flowers include calendula, cosmos, marigold, spider flower, sweet pea, and zinnia. Growing one of these annuals is the best starting point for most gardeners wishing to raise seeds.

If you are noted for a certain crop that does particularly well in your garden, try growing that one for seed first. Peas are a good example, or snap beans. Tomatoes are a good bet for first-time seed savers, too, though remember that hybrids should not be grown for seed. Many flower gardeners start by saving only marigold seeds.

To make your chances of success with vegetables even greater, make your choice from among the self-pollinating annuals, such as snap beans, lettuce, peas, and tomatoes. The term *self-pollinated* means that pollination occurs within each individual, and not from other plants. (More about this in the next chapter.) The reason for choosing a self-pollinating plant is that such plants do not depend on either the wind or insects for assistance in pollination. While insects sometimes do pollinate some of these self-pollinating plants, the problem of isolation, or separation of varieties to avoid crosses, is practically eliminated.

Biennials

Raising seed from biennial vegetables takes a little more persistence. These plants bear their edible crop the season they are planted, waiting until the second season to flower, produce seed, and wither away. Where cold in winter is severe, most biennial vegetables must be dug up in the fall and replanted in the spring. Some of them can be left in the garden and covered with a blanket of hay or leaves, and they will survive to grow seeds.

In all likelihood, you have probably thought of (and grown) these common biennials as annuals. They include beet, Brussels sprout, cabbage, carrot, cauliflower, celeriac, celery, onion, parsley, parsnip, rutabaga, salsify, Swiss chard, and turnip.

During their second growing season, most biennials flower in the spring and ripen their seed in midsummer or late summer. The typical biennial flower grows on a sturdy stalk that originates in the root or leafy crown of the plant. Stalk formation may not be seen, but it is well underway by winter after the plant's first growing season. For a plant to form a good strong seed stalk, the following conditions are usually necessary:

1. The plant should be a mature, well-developed specimen. Small or immature plants may not form seed even if chilled.

2. A chilling period of at least 30 to 60 days, with temperatures no higher than 40° to 50°F. (5° to 10°C.).

3. Moderate weather prevailing during the period of new spring growth in the parent plant.

The biennials pose a new complication for the seed-grower. One must carry the vegetable over the winter in good enough condition so that it will flower and produce seed the following year.

This can be as simple as growing salsify, so hardy that a covering of hay or leaves will protect the roots in the garden during the worst of winters in the North. Or it can be as challenging as growing cauliflower, which in the North will not survive outdoors, and which cannot be stored in a root cellar. Cauliflower must be grown for one season outdoors, then transplanted into a cold frame or greenhouse for the winter, then planted outside again in the spring.

The fall harvest.

Biennial flowers like Canterbury-bells and foxglove overwinter in the garden.

Perennials

Perennials return year after year, growing from underground parts that live over the winter. Most perennials planted from seed will begin to produce seed themselves a year or two after planting. Rhubarb and asparagus are the most frequently grown perennial garden vegetables. There are scores of herbaceous perennial flowers like daylily, iris, delphinium, and peony. New varieties are developed by professional and amateur plant breeders using seeds. These improved varieties are then maintained as true clones of the parent plant using methods of vegetative propagation like division or root cuttings. Describing the techniques of vegetative propagation is beyond the scope of this book; an excellent source for this information is Lewis Hill's *Secrets of Plant Propagation* (Garden Way Publishing, 1985).

CHAPTER 5

Pollination

The little boy had been well satisfied that storks brought babies into the world. But the boy's father felt his son should know more than that, so he gave him a detailed account of the Facts of Life.

The next day the boy's pal asked him where babies came from. "The stork brings them," the boy explained. "But you should have heard the wild story my Dad tried to tell me last night."

Beginning seed growers may share with that boy a desire for simplicity regarding pollination, but they will find nature uncooperative. There is not one simple method, but many. There are self-pollinating flowers, those that cross with other flowers on the same plant, those that cross with others of the same variety, those that cross with other varieties, and many that cross with weeds. The variations seem endless. The seed grower must understand the pollination process of each of the species he or she raises for seeds, or the best efforts will prove futile.

Self-Pollination

A good starting point for understanding pollination (as well as for growing seeds) was suggested in the previous chapter. It's the self-pollinating species. All have what are known as *perfect flowers*, containing both male and female parts.

Such plants as these can be grown fairly close to other varieties of the same plant without fear of crossings, which result in unwanted variations from the parent plant.

The following species are generally self-pollinating:

Pea	Cowpea	Tomato	Clarkia
Snap bean	Endive	Wheat	Sweet pea
Soybean	Oats	Lettuce	Snapdragon

Self-pollination results when the pollen of a flower fertilizes that same flower or another on the same plant.

Cross-Pollination

Cross-pollination results when the pollen from one flower fertilizes a flower on another plant. The pollen is carried either by the wind or by insects, usually bees.

Within this group there are many variations. Some cabbages, for example, have perfect flowers, but flowers that are self-sterile, and thus require the pollen from other plants. This means that the seed grower must not plan to grow cabbage seed by carrying over just a single plant to set out in the spring.

The perfect flower, then, is found in species that cross-pollinate as well as those that self-pollinate. It is found in the orchard (apple, peach, pear, and plum) as well as in the vegetable garden (bean, carrot, celery, eggplant, radish, sweet potato, tomato, pepper, and okra) and the flower garden (sweet alyssum, nicotiana, petunia, salvia, and snapdragon).

Imperfect Flowers

There are certain other flowers that have functional stamens and nonfunctional pistils (called *staminate* or *male flowers*), and flowers with nonfunctional stamens and functional pistils (*pistillate* or *female flowers*). Both of these kinds of flowers are referred to as *imperfect flowers*.

When a plant has *both* staminate and pistillate flowers, it is called a *monoecious* plant (sweet corn, cucumber, cantaloupe, squash, pumpkin, and watermelon, as well as many members of the nut families, including chestnuts, filberts, pecans, and walnuts). When the staminate and pistillate flowers occur on different plants, they are called *dioecious* plants. Holly is probably the best known of this group, which also includes asparagus, date, and persimmon. Spinach produces male plants, female plants, and plants with both male and female flowers.

Some species, particularly in the Aster Family, have compound flowers with combinations of perfect/imperfect and fertile/sterile florets. The single French marigold is an example in which the petal-like ray flowers are pistillate and the disk flowers in the center are perfect.

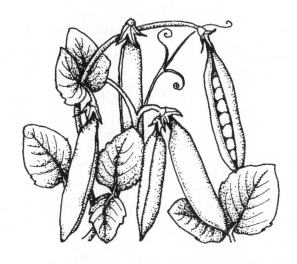

CHAPTER 6

Selecting Seed Parents

Selection of seed is the heart of any garden seed-saving program. If you are careful in choosing the seed that you save from your garden, you can not only perpetuate and multiply your garden plants, but also improve and refine them. Naturally, you will want to save seed from your best plants, since superior plants are more likely to produce seed that will grow into another generation of plants with the same desirable characteristics.

If you intend to save garden seed, don't wait until fall to select the parent plants. Watch your plants throughout the growing season, keeping in mind the qualities you most want to encourage. To select the best plants, you need to know how they've performed all season long.

Consider the Whole Plant

It is the *whole plant*, rather than an isolated individual fruit, that you should consider in making your selection. For example, in choosing a tomato plant, you would want to save seed from a vine that bore many excellent fruits, not simply from one lone huge fruit that caught your eye on the edge of the patch.

The luscious, early-bearing plant that you'd choose first to eat is the one from which you should save seed. That's not always easy to do, especially when the family is clamoring for the first sweet corn. Many gardeners who regularly save seed see enough of an improvement in the plants grown from the seed they select to make the sacrifice worthwhile. If you're not particularly set on cultivating an early strain, though, preferring to select only for flavor or some other quality, or if the species is self-pollinating like tomato, then of course you can go ahead and feast on those very first fruits of your vegetable patch.

If you're saving seed of root crops — carrot, beet, turnip, rutabaga, celeriac, parsnip, salsify — which are biennials, you'll need to dig and store the roots over the winter unless you live in an area where winters are mild. Select the roots for desirable qualities as you pack them away, and then reselect from the stored roots in the spring, choosing for your prime seed stock those that have remained in good shape throughout the storage period. Persons saving potatoes for planting will make the same choices.

You'll have the best luck with cabbage and other brassicas if you let them grow to eating size, or nearly so, before they go through the winter in your garden or cold cellar. Vegetable plants that winter over in an immature state don't always flower and set seed reliably the following spring. Biennial flowers for seed harvest remain in the garden throughout their life cycle.

More Than One

If you intend to save seed from your garden each year, experts advise that you'd be wise to keep seeds from more than one plant of the same variety, even if you only need a few seeds, so that you maintain a broader genetic base for your garden improvement experiments. This is especially true of corn.

There are two exceptions to this rule. Self-pollinated plants such as beans and peas are inbred by nature, and thus all seeds could be saved from one plant without fear of deterioration. If healthy, productive plants are chosen, the seeds should improve in quality. The checklist on page 137 lists common seed-borne diseases to watch for. Rogue out (remove) all diseased seed plants. The second exception is with squashes and pumpkins. Seeds from one squash or pumpkin can be saved without any change in the quality of the plants the following year.

What About Hybrids?

Home gardeners are generally advised not to save seeds from hybrid crops. The offspring of hybrid plants, especially corn, are sometimes sterile. When they do bear fertile seed, that seed will produce plants unlike the parent plant. The product of a cross between hybrid plants often reverts to resemble one of its ancestors.

Since the reason for growing hybrid seed is usually the exceptional vigor to be found in the first generation after the cross, there would be little to gain from breeding hybrids back in the direction of their parent and grandparent plants. There's certainly no harm in saving hybrid seed, though. If you like to experiment, go ahead and plant those seeds. Don't expect great things of this second generation, but keep your eyes open and you might grow something you would enjoy. You shouldn't *depend* on seed saved from a hybrid crop, though, if you want to be sure of harvesting what you need next year.

It's a good idea to keep records, when saving seed, of the kind and number of plants from which you gathered seed, along with any other pertinent data such as yield or earliness notations for the parent plants. This will help you to evaluate the results of your seed-saving efforts after you have been following the practice for a few years.

Plant Qualities

There are many good qualities to look for when selecting plants from which to save seed. You'll want to consider at least some of the following characteristics when choosing your parent plants:

1. Flavor
2. Yield
3. Vigor
4. Color
5. Size
6. Storage life
7. Disease resistance
8. Insect resistance
9. Early bearing (fruits, heads, flowers, etc.)
10. Late in bolting to seed (lettuce, etc.)
11. Good germination in poor weather
12. Absence of thorns, spines, etc.
13. Seeds — few and small in juicy fruits, large for sunflowers, tender for tomatoes.
14. Texture, tenderness, juiciness
15. Suitability for purpose. For example, a paste tomato should be dry and meaty. Flint corn should dry well. Kraut cabbage should be solid. Flowers for cutting should remain erect.
16. Stature — tall, dwarf, intermediate
17. Weather tolerance, drought resistance
18. Aromatic appeal

CHAPTER 7

Collecting Seeds

Once you have selected the plants from which you intend to save seed, your first step is to identify the chosen plants so that they don't accidentally end up in the soup pot or a flower arrangement before you've had a chance to harvest the seed you want. Some gardeners tie a bright cloth or yarn to their elite seed-producing individuals. Others mark the plant with a stake. Be sure that the rest of your family knows which plants should not be picked.

Timing

Your next concern will be to determine the right time to collect the seeds. Seed that is picked too early, before it has had time to mature, will not have had a chance to accumulate enough stored nourishment to get it off to a good start, or even to last it through the winter. Such seed will be likely to be thin and light in weight. It will be less likely to survive storage, to germinate well, or to produce strong seedlings.

So you want your seed to be well ripened before you pick it, but not so far along that it drops onto the ground or gets blown away by the wind.

Generally speaking, seed-bearing garden plants will fall into one of three groups, depending on how they ripen their fruit:

Plants with seeds encased in fleshy fruits, such as tomatoes, eggplants, and peppers. These soft fruits should be allowed to turn fairly ripe, even a bit overripe, before seed is collected. The fruits should be slightly soft, but they should not be so overripe that they begin to heat. It is also important not to allow the fruit to dry around the seed, or it may form a hard covering that will affect the storage life of the seed.

Seed crops, such as corn, wheat, beans, and others in which the seed is the edible part of the plant. Such plants usually hold their seeds for some time after they reach maturity, giving you a chance to do your collecting pretty much when you choose, as long as the seed has become thoroughly dry. Mature plants with dry seeds that tend to bend over in wind or rain may be cut and stacked in a dry place to cure and dry further before removing the seed.

Plants that shatter readily, scattering ripe seed as soon as it reaches maturity. Lettuce, onions, okra, and members of the Mustard Family, as well as many flowers, not only drop their mature seeds promptly as soon as they're dry; they also tend to ripen seed gradually so that a single plant will usually have a good bit of unripe seed hanging on while matured seed is falling off.

To be sure of catching a good seed crop from such plants, you must either inspect them daily and collect ripe seed in small amounts in a paper bag as it becomes ready, or tie a ventilated paper bag over the seed head. The seed that will collect in the bag may still contain some immature specimens, but these can usually be winnowed out by pouring the seed from one container to another in a breeze. Some plants in this group, especially those of the Mustard Family, will need staking to support the seed stalk. When collecting most seeds, try to do the job on a dry, sunny day after dew has evaporated. However, seed from plants in group three above are often collected while damp to avoid seed loss. Although most of the seeds that you'll harvest in the fall will not be hurt by the low temperature of a light frost, the frost can cause an accumulation of moisture that will lower seed quality.

To prevent confusion, label each batch of seeds as soon as possible after collecting, especially if you're saving more than one variety of a species, such as several varieties of tomatoes or peppers or several different members of the Mustard Family, whose seeds are much alike.

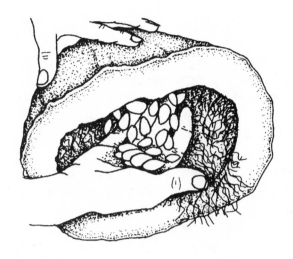

CHAPTER 8

Extracting and Drying Seeds

Your first job, after collecting seed-containing fruits such as tomatoes, peppers, squash, and melons, is to separate the seed from
the pulp. Scrape out the seedy part of the fruit and save the rest of
the overripe flesh for your hens or put it on the compost pile. It's a
good idea to let the tomato seeds and pulp ferment for three or four
days, to help control bacterial canker. To do this, spoon the seedy
tomato pulp into a jar, add about ¼ cup of water, and watch, over
the next few days, as the lightweight pulp and worthless seeds rise to
the top and the heavier, good seeds sink to the bottom.

Some gardeners allow cucumber and melon seeds to ferment, too, using the same procedure. You can also fork out the seeds and wash them.

For squash and pumpkins, separate the seeds from the pulp, wash them thoroughly to remove all traces of vegetable matter, and spread them out to dry. Large seeds should dry for five to six days. Smaller ones may be ready in three or four days.

Peas, beans, soybeans, and limas are usually removed from the dry pods by threshing. Don't be *too* rough on these seeds, though. Internal injuries to the seed are more likely with machine processing, but they *can* happen when force is used to remove seeds from their husks. Damage to the seed may not be noticeable, but if the embryonic stem or root is bruised, the seed may germinate poorly or produce stunted seedlings.

Seed of lettuce, sunflower, dill, calendula, and other plants that are picked dry may be shaken through a screen of hardware cloth to sift out chaff.

Further removal of undesirable lightweight seeds and stem and leaf parts, as well as pulp, may be accomplished by floating them off. When you put the seeds in water, the chaff, "dud" seeds, and pulp will rise to the top and the good seeds will sink to the bottom. Seeds other than tomatoes that you treat in this way should be promptly spread out for drying.

Moisture Content

As already mentioned, excess moisture in the seed will lower its quality. Seed that is not dry enough when stored will keep poorly and have a low percentage of germination. A moisture content of over 20 percent will cause bulk-stored seed to heat. Most seeds fare best when stored with a moisture content of 8 to 15 percent. It is important to thoroughly dry *all* seed that you will store — even already dry-looking seeds like dill and carrot.

You won't be able to tell the exact moisture content of the seed under home conditions, of course, but you *can* give your seeds a long, thorough drying period before you store them, and that should be enough. The important thing to remember is not to package any harvested seed until it has had at least a few days of further air drying after being removed from the plant. The larger the seed, the longer the drying period required.

Most seeds, in most climates, will dry adequately for home storage if spread on paper towels or newspapers in an airy place for a week. They should be turned and possibly spread on fresh dry paper (depending on the kind of seed) several times during that period.

If you were forced to collect your seed during damp weather, or if you live in a humid climate, you might want to use gentle heat to dry some of your seeds like corn and other grains. Such heat must be regulated, though, so that it *never* rises above 100°F. (38°C.), and 90°F. (32°C.) is preferable. Too-rapid drying can cause shrinking and cracking of the seed and formation of a hard, impervious, and undesirable seed coat. Drying at too high a temperature will adversely affect the viability and vigor of the seed.

A far safer method of hastening the drying process is to spread the seed in the sun, on screens or on a flat roof or pavement, for a day or two of intensive drying.

Many seed savers use silica gel (available at many pharmacies or at camera supply, craft, or hardware stores) as a seed desiccant. Enclose the air-dried seeds in a tight container with an equal weight of silica gel. Most silica gel is treated to turn color when it has absorbed its maximum of moisture. The silica gel can be redried in the oven for reuse.

Once the seeds have been dried, do not allow them to sit around in the open air, or they will reabsorb moisture from the ambient humidity.

CHAPTER 9

Storing Seeds

Now that you've grown, selected, picked, and dried your seeds, it's time to store them. Improperly dried seeds may deteriorate drastically over the winter. If you're counting on home-saved seed for your spring plantings, or trying to carry on an heirloom strain of a certain vegetable, the loss of a year's crop of seed can be disastrous.

Seeds, you remember, carry on their basic life processes even while dormant, but at a very low rate. The moisture they absorb from the air combines with stored nourishment to form a soluble food, which then combines with oxygen from the air to release carbon dioxide, water, and heat.

Since your seeds are exchanging elements and gases with the atmosphere while they are dormant, your aim in storing them should be to confine those exchanges to the minimum necessary to sustain life in the seed. That means avoiding any stimulation that would encourage the seed to speed up its metabolism, or that would deteriorate the embryo. So your stored seeds must be protected from moisture and heat, as well as from insects and other animals that would like to eat them.

Moisture

Let's consider moisture first. As mentioned above, the presence of moisture triggers the formation of soluble compounds in the plant. Too much moisture in the air will cause the seed to burn up its stored food at too fast a rate, producing excess heat which further lowers the seed's ability to germinate.

How much dampness is too much? Seeds differ, according to their variety, in their ability to absorb water from the air, even under the same conditions of temperature and humidity. Beans, peas, and cereals (including corn) should contain no more than 13 percent moisture for safe storage. Soybeans should have a little less — 12.5 percent — and peanuts and most other vegetables even less moisture — around 9 percent, with 4 to 6 percent being considered ideal for long-term storage.

According to seed expert Dr. James Harrington, each 1 percent reduction in seed moisture, under 14 percent but not below 5 percent, doubles the life expectancy of most vegetable seeds. Lowering the moisture content below 1 to 2 percent impairs the viability of the seed. You're not likely to get your seeds that dry unless you apply artificial heat. Even though we home gardeners have no way of accurately determining a seed's moisture content, we can use these figures as a guide.

Once the seed has been dried for storage, it should be kept as dry as possible. If seeds are allowed to become damp after the initial drying, they will lose some of their longevity, even if redried. Sealed, moisture-proof containers such as cans and jars are the best place to keep your seeds, but only if the seed is good and dry before it is put away. Damp seeds, stored in covered containers, deteriorate more quickly than dry ones in open storage.

Silica gel can be used in the permanent storage container — equal parts by weight of seeds and silica. Many gardeners place seed in well-marked paper envelopes and store them in tight containers with the silica gel loose on the bottom.

Temperature

Storage temperature also affects the keeping quality of seeds. Most seeds can tolerate cold and even freezing conditions that would kill the parent plant, sometimes as low as 0°F. (–18°C.), as long as they are thoroughly dry. Excess moisture in a seed that is subjected to freezing temperatures may freeze and damage the seed.

Dr. Harrington has found that, at 70 percent relative humidity or lower, it is possible to double the life of the seed for each 9°F. (5°C.) decrease in temperature within the range of 32° to 112°F. (0° to 44.5°C.)

It follows, then, that *heat* — especially when combined with high humidity — is the enemy of seed quality. High temperatures not only speed up the seed's rate of internal chemistry; they also promote activity of fungi, bacteria, and insects that further impair the seed's viability by adding heat from their respirations and sometimes by excreting chemicals or other by-products that harm the embryo or soften the seed coat.

Fungi thrive in 13 to 16 percent moisture at temperatures of 85° to 95°F. (30° to 35°C.) They slow down at 70°F. (21°C.) and barely exist at 50°F (10°C.) Different bacteria thrive at different temperatures, but all of them need a moisture content of 18 percent or so to do much damage. So, to discourage these microorganisms, keep your stored seeds dry and cool.

Long-term storage in the refrigerator or freezer is your best bet, so long as the moisture content of the seed is low and the container that you use is vapor-proof. When removing seeds from cold storage, leave the container closed while the seeds warm to room temperature, or condensation will form on the seeds.

Insects

Invasive insects may be kept out by storing seeds in tightly closed containers. If insect eggs are already present in seeds, they may be discouraged by maintaining a temperature no higher than 40° to 50°F. (5° to 10°C.), at which level most insects that would be likely to affect the seed would be relatively inactive. Freezing, of course, destroys or totally immobilizes insects.

From the preceding sections, you can see that the viability of a seed, far from being an absolute value, depends heavily on conditions of storage — not only during the first year, but throughout the life of the seed. For example, onion seed, usually considered to be short-lived, has been kept for up to 12 years when dry and well sealed, but it goes bad in a few months when stored at high temperatures in a damp place.

Points to Remember

To obtain the best results with your stored garden seeds, you will want to do the following:

1. Store only thoroughly dried seed.

2. Don't allow seed to become damp after the initial drying.

3. Keep the storage temperature as low as possible.

4. Keep the storage area as dry as possible, especially if the temperature is below freezing.

5. Label all containers with variety, date, and any other

pertinent information about the strain you're saving.

6. If you keep seed in envelopes, store the whole collection in a tightly covered lard can, large mayonnaise jar (often available from restaurants), or other sealed container.

7. Peas and beans are best stored in bags rather than in airtight containers.

8. If you keep seeds for more than one year, be sure to protect them as much as possible from heat and dampness during the summer.

From these guidelines, you can see that an ideal place for storing seed is your refrigerator or freezer.

The refrigerator, too, is an excellent place to store those commercial seeds left over from summer gardening activities. Place the envelopes of seeds in a canning jar and cap it.

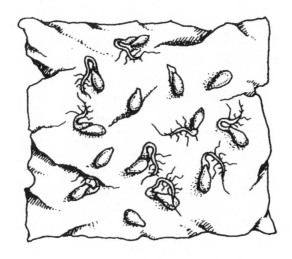

CHAPTER 10

Testing Seeds

The home seed grower will want to provide ideal storage conditions for the seed so that germination rates will be high when the seeds are planted, and so that the seeds can be carried over for more than one year. For example, one should be able to grow a supply of carrot seeds that will last for several years, having gone to the trouble of spending two years in getting the supply. In this way one can make more profitable use of both land and time.

Germination Test

The sure test of success in storing seeds is the *germination test*. This test can be made indoors, before the regular growing season begins, and thus you can avoid the possibly unprofitable use of land in testing the seed. A good germination test provides seeds with ideal conditions of moisture, air, temperature, and light (or darkness). A good general method is to randomly select 10 to 100 seeds of the lot to be checked. Spread the seeds out on a damp paper towel. Place a slip of paper with the date and variety name *penciled* on it with the seeds. Roll up the towel, make it thoroughly moist, and seal it in a polyethylene bag (pervious to air, but not to water vapor). There should not be a puddle of water in the bag. Place the bag in a warm area (approximately 70°F., or 21°C.). Check occasionally to make sure that the towel remains damp. The same bag can be used to hold several towels.

Some seeds such as radishes will germinate in as little as three days, but many will take as long as a week, and some herb seeds take even longer. Be guided by the directions for growing the particular plant.

When the seeds have sprouted, it's time to make your count. Divide the number of seeds germinated by the total number tested, and the result is the percentage of germination. (For example, if you tested 50 seeds and 45 germinated, divide 45 by 50 and the answer is .90, or 90 percent.)

The answer you get can be useful in two ways:

1. It tells you whether your seeds are worth planting.

2. If they are, it gives you an indication of how thickly you should plant them, with a heavier planting indicated if the percentage is low.

For some plants, like peas, the germination test seedlings can be planted in the garden. Your germination tests will most likely take place before the normal growing season (and thus, growing conditions may not favor other crops), but peas are often planted earlier than other vegetables anyway.

Getting Started

You have now completed the basic reading on growing and saving seeds. School's out. It's recess time. Time to get into the garden, to make mistakes and learn from them, to grow and harvest your own seeds, and to experience the rich sense of satisfaction that is in store for you.

Part II of this book deals with growing specific vegetables for seeds. You would expect, perhaps, that it would be written from A to Z, beginning with asparagus, and ending with that prolific friend of all gardeners, the zucchini.

Instead, it's broken down by those various botanical families with the unpronounceable names. Why? Simply because it is easier to understand about growing seeds if all members of a family are considered together. There's much in common, for example, about growing cabbages and broccoli and Brussels sprouts, so much of the material doesn't have to be repeated if they are put together.

Part III covers annual and biennial flowers. These are arranged alphabetically by their accepted common names. All scientific names are based on *Hortus Third,* the primary authority on horticultural nomenclature in North America, and on the *International Code of Botanical Nomenclature.*

Don't be afraid to wander back into the preceding "school-room" pages occasionally. You'll probably want to refer to this basic information over and over as you get started in seed saving.

PART II
THE
VEGETABLES

TABLE I

Characteristics of Common Vegetables Saved for Seed

Vegetable	Page	Life Cycle for Seeds	Seed Viability* (Years)	How Pollinated	Need Isolation
Asparagus	58	Perennial	3	Insect	Yes
Bean	98	Annual	3	Self	Limited
Beet	68	Biennial	4	Wind	Yes
Broccoli	80	Annual	5	Insect	Yes
Brussels Sprouts	81	Biennial	5	Insect	Yes
Cabbage	75	Biennial	5	Insect	Yes
Carrot	104	Biennial	3	Insect	Yes
Cauliflower	81	Biennial	5	Insect	Yes
Celeriac	108	Biennial	5	Insect	Yes
Celery	109	Biennial	5	Insect	Yes
Chinese Cabbage	82	Annual	5	Insect	Yes
Chive	60	Perennial	2	Insect	Yes
Corn, Sweet	54	Annual	1-2	Wind	Yes
Cowpea	102	Annual	3	Self	Limited
Cucumber	126	Annual	5	Insect	Yes
Eggplant	112	Annual	5	Self	Limited
Garlic	61	Annual		See listing	No
Horseradish	89	Perennial		See listing	No
Jerusalem Artichoke	134	Perennial		See listing	No
Kale	85	Biennial	5	Insect	Yes
Kohlrabi	85	Biennial	5	Insect	Yes
Leek	61	Biennial	3	Insect	Yes

TABLE I **51**

Vegetable	Page	Life Cycle for Seeds	Seed Viability* (Years)	How Pollinated	Need Isolation
Lettuce	131	Annual	5	Self	Limited
Lima Bean	101	Annual	3	Self	Limited
Muskmelon	128	Annual	5	Insect	Yes
New Zealand Spinach	74	Annual	5	Wind	Yes
Okra	103	Annual	2	Self	Limited
Onion	63	Biennial	1-2	Insect	Yes
Parsley	110	Biennial	2	Insect	Yes
Parsnip	111	Biennial	1-2	Insect	Yes
Pea	95	Annual	3	Self	Limited
Peanut	98	Annual	1-2	Self	Limited
Pepper	114	Annual	4	Self	Limited
Popcorn	57	Annual	1-2	Wind	Yes
Potato	116	Annual		Self	No
Pumpkin	126	Annual	5	Insect	Yes
Radish	90	Annual	5	Insect	Yes
Rhubarb	66	Perennial		See listing	No
Rutabaga	88	Biennial	5	Insect	Yes
Salsify	134	Biennial	2	Self	No
Soybean	102	Annual	3	Self	Limited
Spinach	72	Annual	5	Wind	Yes
Squash, Summer	120	Annual	5	Insect	Yes
Squash, Winter	120	Annual	5	Insect	Yes
Swiss Chard	71	Biennial	4	Wind	Yes
Tomato	116	Annual	4	Self	Limited
Turnip	87	Annual	5	Insect	Yes
Watermelon	130	Annual	5	Insect	Yes

As reported by authorities. Ideal storage techniques can significantly prolong seed viability.

Monocotyledoneae

The monocotyledons or *monocots,* are a subclass of plants that share the common characteristic of having only one seed leaf (see p. 12). The monocotyledons include the members of the Grass Family and the Lily Family.

Poaceae
GRASS FAMILY

The members of this family are found throughout the world, and they include all of our cereals, the grasses of our lawns and pastures, the treelike bamboos, the sugar cane that produces so much of our sugar — and many of our weeds.

The most popular member of this family found in our vegetable gardens is corn, one of the New World's greatest contributions to agriculture.

Don't be afraid to try corn, just because some method of isolation may have to be used to keep the seed from being the result of a cross. It's possible to get both earlier corn and better-tasting corn by raising your own seeds. Remember to save for seed the earliest corn that is well developed and has full-grained ears.

CORN, SWEET (*Zea mays* var. *rugosa*). Annual. Monoecious. Has male (the tassel) and female (ears) flowers on each plant. Wind-pollinated.

Grow only standard (open-pollinated, not hybrid) varieties for seed. These include Golden Midget (yellow, early), Golden Bantam (very sweet, yellow, midseason), Country Gentleman (white, late, and does not have regular rows of kernels), and Stowell's Evergreen (white, late).

Plant in hills (start six seeds per hill, cut back to three plants per hill) or rows (final spacing, 12 inches). Corn is a hungry crop. Furnish plenty of nitrogen-rich fertilizer to provide for the healthy plants that will produce the best seeds. Pollination will be better if planting is in four or more adjacent rows.

To maintain variety purity, ears to be saved for seed must be isolated. Remember that sweet corn will cross with popcorn, flint corn, and field corn as well as with other varieties of sweet corn. Three ways to isolate corn are:

By distance. The distance downwind from the nearest crop of a different variety is most important. A distance of 1,000 feet between varieties is recommended for absolute purity, though 250 feet is far enough if some crossing can be tolerated.

By time. Make certain the yellow pollen of the other varieties is not being spread when the silk of the corn to be saved is developing. Planting seeds at different times may achieve this.

By isolating the developing ears to be saved. If there are gardens near yours, this is the only reliable system for the gardener saving seeds. Obtain a supply of bags that are water-resistant, but not plastic. One should be placed over each ear to be saved, before the silk can be seen. Tie it in place. You may have to replace bags one or more times as rains disintegrate them.

When the pollen can be seen on the tassels, cut off one. Remove the bag from an ear on a different plant, and rub the silk with the tassel. Then replace the bag. Do this to all of the ears being saved.

These ears must be protected from unwanted pollen until the silk turns brown. After the bags are removed, tie pieces of woolen yarn around the ears to be saved, to identify them so they will not be gathered and eaten with the rest of the crop.

No matter how modest your demands for seed, treat at least 12 to 15 ears in this fashion. This will permit you to rogue (discard) any ears with undesirable traits and to save seeds with a broad genetic background, thus avoiding unwanted inbreeding.

The gardener should inspect both plants and ears before selecting the ears to be saved. One may wish to save the earliest ears, those from plants with the greatest productivity, or those that show a resistance to very dry conditions. Choosing the fullest, most perfect ears from the earliest-bearing plants is recommended.

The ears should be left on the plants about a month later than the remainder of the crop picked for eating. While frost will not damage the seed if the ears are dry and mature, the ears should be picked before hard freezes, which could reduce the percentage of germination. Further drying will be necessary. Strip back the husks, then tie or braid several ears together. Hang them up in your home. They will dry and, at the same time, pro-

The tassel, at top, provides the pollen for the female flowers, the silks of the ears.

Corn to be dried and saved for seeds.

vide a rustic decoration during the holiday season.

Shelling is a splendid job for winter evenings. It involves twisting off the kernels and discarding the ones at the end of the ear that are not completely developed.

Since corn is usually considered viable for only one to two years, most gardeners will find it wise to raise seed corn annually.

POPCORN (*Zea mays* var. *praecox*). Follow directions for sweet corn. Remember that, as with sweet corn, there are both hybrid and open-pollinated varieties; select the latter for seed saving. Japanese Hulless and Strawberry are two popular varieties.

Shelling popcorn can injure the hands. Try rubbing the ears against one another to make the shelling easier.

Liliaceae
LILY FAMILY

The Easter lily and the many other lilies that decorate our flower gardens and homes belong to this family, and so do tulips, the tiny lily-of-the-valley, and, most important for vegetable gardeners, the onion and asparagus.

Growing asparagus from seeds takes time, but certainly is possible. Four other members of this family are excellent for the beginner who wishes to experiment with propagation. Success is almost assured. Garlic is foolproof, since no seeds are involved. There are no isolation problems with leeks or chives, and both of these, as well as onions, are tolerant about storage conditions, with leeks and chives remaining in the ground, and onions needing only a cool, dry storage place, between the first and second year of growth.

ASPARAGUS *(Asparagus officinalis)*. Perennial. Dioecious (male and female plants). Pollinated by insects.

Raising asparagus from seed requires patience. The crop cannot be harvested for three years, or one more than is required if roots are planted.

Female plants produce red berries, which should be gathered in the fall before the first frost. If you are handling small quantities, put the berries in a cloth bag, then crush them by stepping on the bag. Put the mass of seed-pulp into a pail or bowl of water and wash it. The pulp and unwanted light seeds will float to the top and should be discarded. The seeds at the bottom are saved. Dry them for several days by spreading them out and turning them over occasionally, then store them.

Take advantage of advances in the development of varieties by selecting seeds from the rust-resistant Mary Washington or Martha

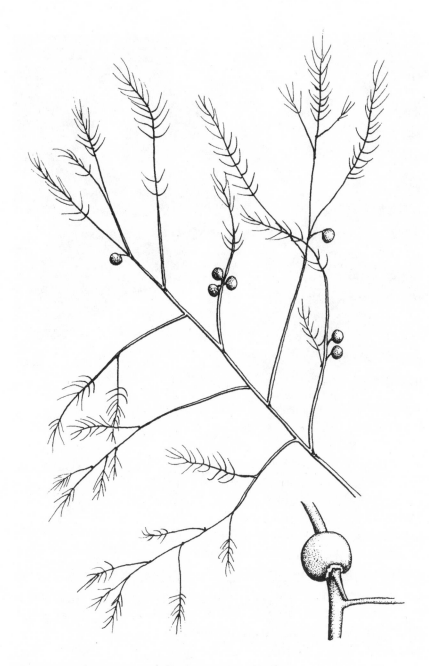

Berries found on the female asparagus plants.

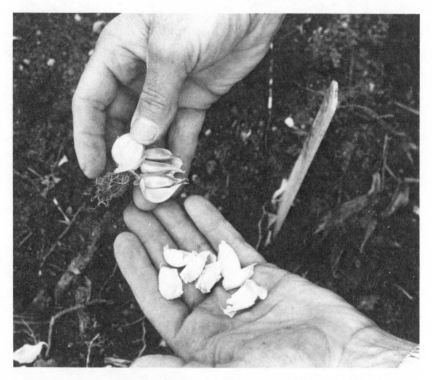

A garlic bulb divided into cloves for planting.

Washington varieties. While bees do carry the asparagus pollen, unwanted cross-pollination is rarely a problem for the home gardener because of the few varieties grown. Commercial growers strive for a mile between plantings to assure purity.

CHIVE *(Allium schoenoprasum)*. Perennial. Pollinated by bees. The chive makes a decorative plant for flower gardens and borders with its tiny rose-purple flowers. If flowers and seed are desired, the clumps of chives, of course, cannot be cut back for use in the kitchen. The seed, black and smaller than onion seed, should be harvested when it can be seen, so it will not be lost through shattering. Home gardeners need not worry about undesirable cross-pollination. For harvesting, drying, and storing, see Onion. Chives are also easily propagated by division of clumps.

GARLIC *(Allium sativum).* Garlic is propagated by dividing the bulbs and planting the individual cloves.

LEEK *(Allium ampeloprasum,* Porrum Group). Biennial. Pollinated by bees. Seeds form in the second year.

Plants are cultivated as for harvesting the first year. Even in northern climates the plants do not have to be stored, but may be left in the

The umbel of the leek, found in the second year of growth.

The umbel of an onion plant.

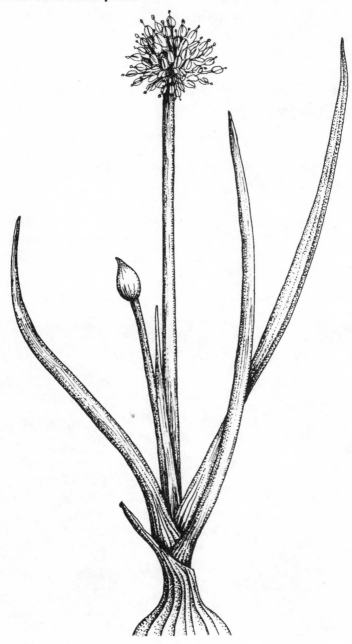

ground. The fall period is an excellent time for the home gardener to rogue out (and eat) the less desirable plants, marking the best for seed production. If you fear the plants will not survive the winter, hill them up with soil, or mulch them with hay or leaves. The second year, the individual plants will send up single stalks four to five feet high, each capped with an enormous ball (it's an *umbel,* composed of hundreds of flowers). Pick the umbels in the fall, and dry them well. The seeds are contained in capsules, and brisk rubbing of the heads is needed to extract the seeds. For other harvesting and drying details, see Onion.

ONION *(Allium cepa).* Biennial. Pollinated by bees. Coal-black seed forms in the second year.

To insure purity of variety, onions must be isolated from other varieties in their second year of growth by a distance of a quarter mile. However, the gardener need not worry about onions being grown for eating (and thus in the first year of growth), since cross-pollination can only occur between flowering plants.

Like onions being grown for home consumption, onions being grown for seed may be started from seeds, sets, or plants. There are two methods of growing them:

Bulb-to-seed. Most home gardeners will practice this method, growing onions as they would for eating: harvesting and storing them, then replanting them the second year. This gives the gardener an opportunity to select the best onions for planting the following year, and roguing out for eating the ones with such undesirable traits as thick necks or double-onions. This method is used in milder climates, where onions are planted in the fall, harvested the following year, rogued, and immediately replanted; as well as in colder areas, where the onions are planted as early in the spring as possible, harvested and rogued in the fall, stored in a cool (32° to 40°F. or 0° to 5°C.), dry room, then replanted as soon as the ground can be worked in the spring.

Seed-to-seed. This method means planting seed and letting plants remain in soil through the second year until the seeds are harvested. This reduces the labor involved, and the expense, and is better for those onions that do not store well, such as some of the sweet onions.

When using the first method, the onions should be planted (in the second year) three to four inches apart, in rows three feet apart. They will send up stalks as high as four feet, capped by the flowers that produce the seeds. For the second method, thin the onions the second year to three to four inches apart in rows three feet apart.

Some experts advise making a cut down into the top of the onion before replanting it, to hasten the development of the stalk. There is general agreement that the larger onion produces more seed.

The heads should be watched from midsummer on. When the black seeds can be seen, start the harvest, cutting off the seed heads and a piece of the stem. Several cuttings may be required, since all seeds will not be ready for harvesting at the same time. Do not save seed from precocious bolters. Dry the heads, then flail them to remove the seeds. If there is a great deal of debris in the seeds, place them in water, so that the debris will float, while the seeds sink. Do not allow seeds to soak for any length of time. Dry them well and store them.

Dicotyledoneae

The dicotyledons or *dicots,* are plants having two cotyledons or seed leaves (see p. 12). They include most of the common vegetables, except asparagus, onions (and onion relatives), and corn.

Polygonaceae
BUCKWHEAT OR RHUBARB FAMILY

This family includes two members of particular interest to the home gardener.

One is buckwheat, which may be grown, not to harvest, but to till under to improve the soil. Raising two consecutive crops of buckwheat in a garden is an excellent way to discourage future weed growth. The buckwheat should be turned under not later than the flowering stage to avoid an unwanted future crop.

The second important member of this family for the home gardener is rhubarb.

RHUBARB *(Rheum rhabarbarum).* Perennial. Cross-pollinated. Pollinated by insects. Grows best in northern states.

Propagation by division of the crown is strongly recommended, since seeds may not produce plants that are true to the variety.

When planning a bed of rhubarb, select a site that will not interfere with production of annual crops in your garden. Along one side of the garden is preferred. Soil should be prepared by the addition of compost, plant foods, or manure. In early spring, dig up the crown of a large parent plant, cut off several chunks for propagating, then replant the original plant. The crowns cut off should be placed about four feet apart, at the same depth as they were found on the parent plant. Six plants will provide ample rhubarb for a family.

Those who wish to try saving rhubarb seeds should let the tall center stalk of the plant grow in the summer. Cut off the top of the stalk when the seeds are mature (dry and flaky), then separate and dry the seeds. Plant them the following spring, thinning them to three to four inches apart when they emerge from the soil. The following spring, select plants wanted for production, and replant them four feet apart in rows six feet apart.

Dividing existing plants is preferable to growing rhubarb from seed, since it not only ensures you will get the variety you want, but because it benefits the original (mother) plant, which can continue to produce vigorously for as long as 20 years. If you are not growing rhubarb for seed, be sure to cut back the seed stalk, to conserve the food supply of the plant for greater stalk production the following year.

The seed stalk of the rhubarb, with its multitude of seeds at the top.

Chenopodiaceae
GOOSEFOOT FAMILY

The three members of the Goosefoot Family described below vary considerably in the work that is involved in obtaining seed from them. Spinach is all too eager to go to seed, and does so the same year it is planted. The home gardener must wait two years for seed from Swiss chard, but growing it is relatively easy, since throughout the United States chard is hardy enough to remain in the garden through the winter, in colder climates asking only for a winter coat of mulch for protection. Beets, also biennial, are more difficult to raise for seed since, in all but the most moderate of climates, the beets must be gathered and stored for the winter. For the beginning seed saver, spinach is a good vegetable to try, particularly if the problems of isolation are not insurmountable. The growing of beet seeds, however, is best left to the more experienced seed grower.

BEET (*Beta vulgaris*, Crassa Group). Biennial. Perfect flowers (having both male and female parts). Cross-pollinated, with extremely light pollen often carried for miles by winds.

The beet produces the familiar rosette of leaves the first year, but the second year produces a seed stalk several feet high. This has branches, along which tiny blossoms appear, followed by the beet "seed" — actually corky seed balls containing enough seeds to produce up to six plants.

Here are two methods for growing beet seeds, which are also used for many of the other biennial vegetables:

Root-to-seed. Home gardeners, particularly in the North, should try this method, growing the beets as if for the kitchen, but planting them later in the season, so the beets reach only a moderate size (one to two inches in diameter) at fall harvesting time. During the growing season, plants with undesirable traits such as poor leaf quality should be pulled, and the thinnings used for beet greens.

In the fall, the beets should be pulled. The beets with the most desirable characteristics in terms of color, shape, and size should be saved for seed plants, with the remainder used for eating. The tops of those saved for seed should be cut, but not closer than one inch from the top of the beets. Handle the beets carefully; damaged beets will rot. About half a dozen beets will provide more than enough seeds for home needs, but you will want to save more than this, in case some of them do not winter-over well.

Many storage systems are effective. Ideal temperatures are 40° to 50°F. (5° to 10°C.), or about what is found in many "unheated" basements or root cellars.

Try storing beets in a box, placing a layer of fresh sawdust or sand in the bottom, adding a layer of beets, then another layer of sawdust or sand, and continuing until the box is full. Any storage system should provide some moisture, since a dry, shriveled beet will produce few or no seeds.

In the spring, as soon as the soil can be worked, the beets should be set out, crowns planted barely beneath the soil, with the beets spaced two feet apart in rows three feet apart.

Seed-to-seed. This method requires less work than the previous method and doesn't require storing the beets; on the other hand, the gardener does not have the opportunity to select the best roots for propagation, and the method can be used only in mild climates, since beets are not cold-hardy. Seeds are planted in August to September, with the earlier dates used in the less mild areas, and for slower-growing varieties. Beets get first-year growth in the fall, and can be mulched if the gardener knows such protection is needed. In the second year, the beets should be thinned to permit a space of two feet between plants, in rows three feet apart. Most gardeners who have raised beets only for eating and have never seen the second-year growth, are surprised at the height, width, and quality of this seed-stalk growth.

These beets are an ideal size to save for growing seed.

Don't attempt seed crops of both beets and Swiss chard in the same season. The two will cross (and both will cross with sugar beets). You can, of course, have first-year crops of both, or a seed crop of one and a first-year crop of the other. Similarly, you should not attempt seed crops of more than one variety of either beets or Swiss chard in the same year. Commercial growers strive for at least a mile's distance between seed crops of Swiss chard and beets, or between different varieties of either vegetable. The home gardener, of course, cannot plan for such spaciousness, but can take comfort in the knowledge that few home gardeners grow either Swiss chard or beets as biennials for seed, and thus the chances of stray air-borne pollen causing unwanted cross-pollination are relatively small. Because both beet and Swiss chard seeds will remain viable for four or more years if given reasonable treatment, the gardener can alternate years in growing these two vegetables for seed, and thus always have enough seed for home use.

When some of the seeds have reached maturity (they will be brown), cut the entire plants at ground level and hang them upside down in a dry, protected area such as a garage or barn. When the plants are dry, seed balls are easily stripped by hand from the branches. If only a few beets are being raised for seeds, a convenient method for collecting the seeds straight from the garden is to bend each stalk into a large grocery bag and strip off the seeds that are brown and mature. This can be repeated later when more seeds have matured.

If considerable debris is stripped off with the seed balls, the seeds should be cleaned by winnowing. Use a wooden salad bowl for this, placing the seed in the bowl on a breezy day, then tossing the seed gently into the air until the lighter chaff has blown away.

SWISS CHARD (*Beta vulgaris,* Cicla Group). Biennial. Perfect flowers (having both male and female parts). Cross-pollinated, by wind.

Swiss chard and beets are very similar, except that Swiss chard is grown for its foliage, while beets are grown for their roots and, increasingly, for the immature plant, from which both roots and foliage are eaten.

Gardeners can grow Swiss chard by either method listed under beets. There is one big difference, though: Swiss chard is extremely hardy, so there is no need to dig up and store the plants as described under Method 1. The plants are left in the ground (in extremely cold areas, they can be heavily mulched after the first few frosts), then dug up and transplanted in the spring, at about one foot apart in rows three feet apart. Since the foliage is the part of Swiss chard that is eaten, the gardener need not inspect the roots when roguing out undesirable plants. For this reason, many home gardeners may favor Method 2. It may be necessary to stake up the seed stalks as they reach maturity.

Gardeners should be aware that there are both white-stemmed and red-stemmed varieties of Swiss chard. The latter is often called "rhubarb chard." While the two varieties taste alike, many gardeners choose it because of its greater ornamental value.

SPINACH *(Spinacia oleracea).* Annual. Cross-pollinated. Pollen carried by wind.

The various curiosities found in the reproductive patterns of plants are well illustrated in the spinach plant. Within one row in your garden you may find four distinct types of plants. The one most desired for both harvesting and seed production is the *monoecious* plant, which bears both male and female flowers (see p. 25). Satisfactory, too, are the female plant, having only pistillate flowers, and with foliage that is fine for harvesting, and the vegetative male, with staminate flowers and edible foliage. Unwanted and discarded as soon as they are recognized are the extreme male plants, smaller than the others and having staminate flowers and few or no leaves.

The tendency to produce seed early, a desired characteristic in many vegetables, is not wanted in spinach, since the emergence of the seed stalk marks the end of the crop as a desirable food plant. Thus, the early bolters in your rows should be eliminated, in an attempt to harvest seed that doesn't have this characteristic. Seed should be harvested from among the plants that were the last to bolt.

Sow seeds of this cold-hardy plant in early spring, or, in milder climates, in the fall, with growth completed the following spring. Plant the seeds in rows two feet apart. As the plants reach about six inches in height, you should, in one operation, weed the seed row to insure good growth, rogue out the stunted male plants (and any others with an undesirable appearance), and thin the plants to about six inches apart, reserving those thinnings for dinner that evening. At least one more roguing will be needed to eliminate the plants that bolt early.

Spinach bolts when temperatures rise and days grow longer. The flowers may not be recognized as such, since, not having to attract insects, they lack petals. As the plants turn yellow, the seeds are reaching maturity. They may be gathered by pulling the plants, then stripping the seeds from the stalk with your hands.

Maintaining purity of variety in spinach can be nearly impossible in some home gardens, particularly where many varieties are being grown by neighbors and allowed to bolt, thus spreading the

The late-bolting spinach plants should be saved for growing seeds.

dustlike pollen over a vast area. If there are only a few gardeners in your immediate area, perhaps you can get your neighbors to agree on a variety that everyone will grow. Otherwise the chances of growing a pure strain are slight; the seed grower can only rogue out any undesirable plants that grow the following year from the seed he has grown, and expect to purchase commercially grown seed and try again after a few years.

Tetragoniaceae
NEW ZEALAND SPINACH FAMILY

This family consists of over 50 herbs and small shrubs, including one common vegetable, New Zealand spinach.

NEW ZEALAND SPINACH *(Tetragonia expansa)*. Annual. Wind-pollinated.

This delightful substitute for spinach will grow and prosper in temperatures that would make spinach bolt.

Since the time required to produce seed is long, start plants indoors in a cold frame. Plant outside when all danger of frost is past, 18 inches apart in rows spaced three feet apart. Plants bolt slowly. Flowers develop first at the bottom of the plant, continuing on up the plant.

New Zealand Spinach develops seedpods containing several seeds each. As they mature, they will shatter. Before this happens, cut the plants and place them on a canvas to cure. They can be shaken to dislodge the seed, and the seed can then be gathered.

Brassicaceae
MUSTARD OR CABBAGE FAMILY
(Surface Crops)

The gardener attempting to raise seed of members of the Mustard or Cabbage Family faces two main problems:

Isolation. Broccoli, Brussels sprouts, cabbage, cauliflower, kale, and kohlrabi will all cross with each other if any of them are flowering at the same time. The rule for the gardener should be to have only one of these flowering at a time if one is saving the seed. Similarly you can expect trouble if one of these brassicas is flowering at the same time in a neighbor's garden within 100 yards of your own. Crossing can be expected, too, if two varieties of cabbages are raised within 100 yards of each other.

The flowers are pollinated chiefly by bees. As a rule, bees will not go from one type of plant to another while collecting honey, preferring to collect from only one source, such as apple blossoms or goldenrod, at a time. But in the case of the brassicas, the Mustard Family, the bees do not differentiate between broccoli and cabbage, or any of the others, and will gather from all at the same time.

Commercial growers strive for much more than 100 yards between varieties or between the various members of this family, with one mile given as the minimum distance. Such a distance is impractical for most home gardeners to duplicate.

Biennials. The second problem associated with growing these vegetables for seed is that all of them except broccoli are biennials, requiring two growing seasons to produce seeds, and thus the plants have to be carried through a winter. This can be difficult, particularly in northern areas, and is most difficult with cauliflower.

CABBAGE (*Brassica oleracea,* Capitata Group). Biennial. Perfect flowers (having both male and female parts). Pollinated by bees. May be self-sterile.

Cabbages grown for seed have the usual head the first year, and in the second produce a seed stem with branches. The stem may grow as high as five feet, and should be staked for support. Leaves, much smaller than first-year cabbage leaves, and bright yellow flowers grow on the stem and the many branches. Pods develop, containing up to 20 seeds each. When the pods turn yellow, the seeds are mature. While an individual plant may produce as much as one-half pound of seed, the gardener should raise at least six cabbage plants for seed. Some of the plants may be self-sterile, so a quantity of seeds can be guaranteed only by raising several plants. Cabbage requires a cool period between the two growing seasons to force bolting. The period, studies have shown, can range from about 30 days at temperatures below 50°F. (10°C.) to 60 days at 60°F. (15°C.) or below.

Two methods of growing seed crops are practiced commercially, and can also be used by the home gardener:

Seed-to-seed method. Plants remain in place for two seasons, from the original planting until the seed crop has been harvested. If winter temperatures in your area seldom go below 10°F. (-12°C.), try this method, since it involves less work and avoids the trouble of storing the cabbages through the winter. Plants can be spaced about two feet apart in rows four feet apart, with the small cabbage varieties planted more closely than this.

Time the planting so that the head of the cabbage will not be completely formed at the time of heavy frosts. At this time, shovel soil around the cabbages, three-quarters of the way up the plant's height. This soil can be pulled away from the plants in the spring as soon as the soil can be worked. The uncovered plants will be hardy enough to withstand frosts and even late snows.

A common practice is to slash an inch-deep X across the top of the head, to hasten the emergence of the seed stalk.

When this stalk appears, a stake capable of supporting the five-foot stalk should be driven in beside the plant, and the stalk tied to it. One drawback of this system is that the gardener will tend to raise seed from all the cabbages that survive the winter. One must be particularly alert to rogue out any with undesirable characteristics, to avoid a gradual deterioration of the seed.

Plant-to-seed method. This method involves growing the cabbage

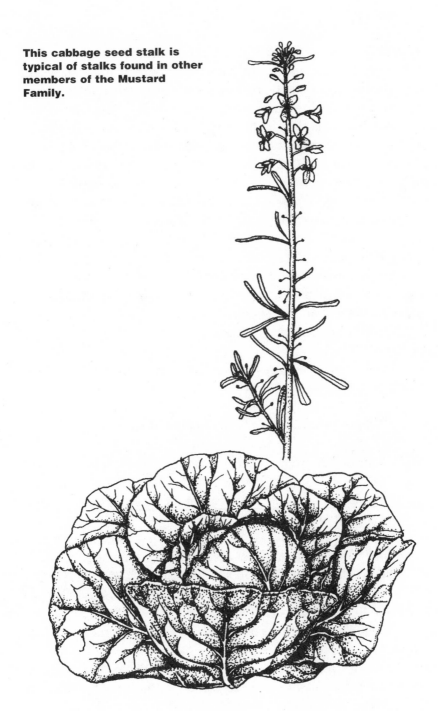

This cabbage seed stalk is typical of stalks found in other members of the Mustard Family.

head, pulling and storing it and its root system over the winter, then replanting it in the spring. The gardener should plant cabbages for seed somewhat later than those one will harvest for eating. The aim is to have the head reach maturity in the late fall, after the first fall frosts, so that it will store well.

To produce more than enough seed for several years, try raising 18 cabbages the first year. This will give you an opportunity to save the 12 best specimens for planting the following year, reserving the others for eating. With any luck you will be able to winter over enough cabbages so that you can select the six best for planting for seed.

When roguing out undesirable plants, remember that the job must be completed before the first blossoms appear on the second-year plants, or else pollen from those undesirable plants may fertilize the plants that are being saved.

Try to store your seed cabbages:

1. Where temperatures will remain as close to 32°F. (0°C.) as possible. This keeps the plant dormant.

2. Where humidity is high, so the plant does not dry out.

3. On shelves, packed closely together, but not piled up.

They should be inspected occasionally during the winter, and any that are rotten should be thrown away.

An ideal storage place is a cold cellar such as is used for storing root crops. Sometimes cabbages are stored in pits and covered with soil. This method provides adequate moisture, and the cabbages will not be harmed if frozen. But there is a greater chance of spoilage going undetected and spreading.

The bulky outer leaves of the cabbage can be removed before storing.

In the spring, as early as the soil can be worked, the cabbage and its root system should be replanted, about two feet apart in

Selecting one of the best cabbages for seed production.

rows four feet apart. The cabbage head should be resting on the ground, several inches lower than it was in its original position.

Cut an inch-deep X in the top of each head, and, when the stalk appears, support it with a stake.

At seed harvesting time, you'll find the cabbages most uncooperative, since all the seeds do not mature at the same time. The seeds are contained in small pods, and the first pods will be turning yellow, then brown, and then *dehiscing* (splitting open and spilling out their seeds), before the last ones have matured. Cut the plants when the pods begin to change color. Dry them in some way so that any seeds falling from shattered pods can be caught. Piling the plants on a large sheet is one way to do this. The immature pods will ripen and turn in color during this drying period. Strip the pods from the branches, place them in a bag or pillowcase, and beat them with your hands.

If many seeds have been grown, the easiest method to clean the chaff from the seeds is to build a screen that will permit these small, round seeds to fall through, but will hold back the trash. Another system, if only a few seeds are grown, is to place the seeds and trash on a slightly inclined plane, such as a table propped up on one side, then work the mass over with your hands, permitting the seeds to roll down and into a container.

The seeds may also be winnowed.

BROCCOLI (*Brassica oleracea,* Botrytis Group). Annual. Has perfect flowers (having both male and female parts). Pollinated by bees. May be self-sterile.

Broccoli is unlike the other members of this family in that it produces flowers the first year. For this reason it is a good plant for the beginner to try. Broccoli will cross with Brussels sprouts, cabbage, cauliflower, kale, and kohlrabi if any of these are flowering at the same time (midsummer) as the broccoli flowers, so the gardener should raise only one of these per year for seed. The edible part of broccoli is the mass of green buds, which eventually develop into tiny yellow flowers.

In colder climates, broccoli grown for seed should be started indoors, in a greenhouse, or in a cold frame, with plants set out two weeks before the last expected frost. Set plants 18 inches apart in rows three feet apart. Rogue out any weak or off-type plants when setting them out, and again before the plants blossom.

In warmer climates, gardeners can sow seeds of the cold-hardy broccoli in the early fall, so that the plants will produce seeds late the following spring.

When most of the seedpods have turned brown and dried, the broccoli plants can be cut. The process of harvesting, threshing, and cleaning is the same as for cabbage seed.

BRUSSELS SPROUTS (*Brassica oleracea,* Gemmifera Group). Biennial. Perfect flowers (having both male and female parts). Some may be self-sterile. Pollinated by bees. See Cabbage entry for problems with crossing.

Nearly all of the directions for cabbage apply to Brussels sprouts. The grower in the North may have difficulty in carrying the plants through the winter because of the tendency of the small cabbage-like sprouts to dry out in storage. The growing of these seeds is much easier in more temperate climates, since the plants are very hardy and will survive in the garden without being uprooted and stored. It is not necessary to slash the tops of the small Brussels sprouts heads to promote growth, as is done with cabbage heads.

CAULIFLOWER (*Brassica oleracea,* Botrytis Group). Biennial. Perfect flowers (having both male and female parts). For crossing dangers, see Cabbage. Pollinated by bees.

Most gardeners consider the cauliflower the fussiest of the Mustard Family to grow, and the most difficult to raise for seed. Beginning seed growers, particularly in the North, should consider the growing of cauliflower seeds an advanced exercise. The problem is in carrying the parent plant over from one growing season to the next.

I have proven to my own satisfaction that in northern Vermont it is impossible to carry the cauliflower over, either by mulching it in the garden or by storing it in a root cellar. Both attempts were made during one winter; both were dismal failures.

Greater success can be achieved by starting the seeds in early September in flats, placed in a cold frame. They are repotted into peat pots about six weeks later, and moved into a cool greenhouse. There they are repotted into larger pots in midwinter, and finally moved into the garden in late April, where they move from the curd (ready-to-eat) stage to the formation of seed stalks.

In warmer climates, such as in California, the seeds are sown in midsummer, and grown on the seed-to-seed plan (see p. 76).

In either case, the spacing should be ample, since the seed stalk, while smaller than the cabbage, requires more room than the first-year plant. Three feet in each direction is the minimum separation distance for most cauliflower varieties.

Like the other brassicas, the cauliflower produces a seed stalk, on which yellow flowers form. The seedpods form in the summer and in the fall turn yellow, then brown. Like cabbage plants, they can be cut and then piled on a sheet to dry further. Follow the directions under Cabbage for harvesting and threshing.

CHINESE CABBAGE (*Brassica rapa,* Pekinensis Group). Annual. Flowers are perfect (having both male and female parts). Pollinated by bees. Self-sterility should be expected.

You might expect that this vegetable would cross with cabbage and other brassicas that we have discussed. But it won't. Instead, it will cross with other varieties of Chinese cabbage, as well as with turnips, radishes, rutabagas, and mustards, both cultivated and wild. Professional growers use one-quarter mile as the minimum isolation distance. The home gardener should grow only one member from this group per season for seed, but can grow all of them as crops for eating. Just make certain that only one will be flowering.

Chinese cabbage, labeled to be saved.

Because Chinese cabbage is an annual, the crops can be sown directly where the seeds will be produced. Space plants 12 to 16 inches apart in rows 30 inches apart.

Gardeners in the North plant Chinese cabbage late, knowing that, if it is planted early or if it is transplanted, it may bolt before forming heads. While this may seem desirable for seed production, it means the cabbage is not heading, and therefore the chance is lost to cull out plants with undesirable characteristics such as loose heads.

The northern gardener has three possible methods of growing this vegetable for seed:

1. As just described, plant early, knowing that the plants will produce seed without producing a head. This assures you of seed, but makes it impossible to rogue to get the best possible heads.

2. Plant as late as mid-June, and thus have the opportu-

nity to rogue out undesirable plants. You will be taking a chance on getting mature seeds before the first heavy frost.

3. Plant in the late summer, mulch the plants after the first heavy frost, and hope that heavy snows will also protect this hardy plant. Then, in the spring, rogue out any undesirable plants as they head.

In areas with milder winters, seed sown in the fall will head, then produce seed stalks and yellow flowers the following spring.

The Chinese cabbage seed stalk is not as large as the cabbage stalk. The seed is found in small pods, and harvesting is the same as for cabbage seed.

Kale, one of the hardiest of all vegetables.

KALE (*Brassica oleracea,* Acephala Group). Biennial. Flowers are perfect (having both male and female parts). Pollinated by bees. May be self-sterile.

Hardiest of the brassicas, kale can be grown even in the North using the seed-to-seed method (see p. 76). Plant as for a food crop, either in early spring or following some other crop in midsummer. In the far North, a mulch applied after the first heavy frosts will give the plants added protection. Plants will produce seed stalks, blossoms, and small seedpods the following summer and fall. Stake up the stalks. For harvesting directions, follow those for Cabbage.

Remember that kale is closely related to broccoli, Brussels sprouts, cabbage, cauliflower, and kohlrabi, and will cross with all the other members of this group.

Because kale is so hardy, it is an excellent choice for the beginner who wishes to raise the seeds of one of the brassicas.

KOHLRABI (*Brassica oleracea,* Gongylodes Group). Biennial. Has perfect flowers (having both male and female parts). Pollinated by bees. May be self-sterile.

Kohlrabi, one of the most unusual members of the Mustard Family, is grown for its ball-like swollen stem.

In more temperate zones, seed is planted in the fall. The following spring, the crop should be carefully inspected, with any plants having other-than-uniform stems of the desired color being rogued out.

In more northern areas, gardeners may choose between mulching the plants after the first heavy frost, then uncovering them in the spring, or pulling up the plants, roots and all, in the late fall, storing them (following the directions in the entry for Cabbage, p. 78), then replanting them in the spring. If you use either of these methods, time your seeding so that the plant's growth will be halted by heavy frosts before the plant has reached full maturity.

The swollen stem is the part of kohlrabi that is eaten.

Since kohlrabi produces an ungainly seed stalk the second year, the home gardener should give the plants ample room, setting them out perhaps 24 inches apart in rows 30 inches apart. Harvesting and storage are the same as for cabbage.

Brassicaceae
MUSTARD OR CABBAGE FAMILY
(Root Crops)

All of these root crops grow best in cool, moist climates. The group whose members will cross with each other includes turnip, radish, rape, mustard, rutabaga, Chinese cabbage (see p. 82), as well as wild varieties of mustard and turnip. The home seed grower should permit only one of these vegetables to flower at any one time in the garden, and should cut back any wild varieties to avoid crosses between them and the vegetable crop. Professional growers set one-quarter mile as the minimum isolation distance between varieties.

TURNIP (*Brassica rapa,* Rapifera Group). Biennial. Perfect flowers (having both male and female parts). Pollinated by bees.

This hardy plant is relatively easy to grow for seed, and so is a good candidate for the beginner who wants to grow seed from one of the biennial brassicas.

The turnip can be grown for seed using one of two methods:

Root-to-seed. This method must be used only in the most northern areas of the country, and involves digging and storing the roots. An advantage of this method is that it permits inspection of the roots, so that those that do not store well, or are not uniform in size, shape, or color can be discarded.

The home gardener using this method will plant for seed much later than for a crop for eating. Time your planting so that the crop will barely reach maturity in late fall. Dig up the roots at this time, or in the early winter. Cut back the turnip tops to one inch from the crowns, then place the roots in damp sand and store them in a near-freezing site, such as a root cellar. (If you have a tried-and-true method for storing carrots, for eating during the winter, use it for storing turnips.)

In the spring, as early as the ground can be worked, set the roots out, with the crowns at ground level, 18 inches apart in rows spaced two feet apart.

Seed-to-seed. This method can be used throughout most of the country, and even in cold areas if snows are heavy enough to protect the roots during the winter. While roguing to discard roots that are not uniform in shape, size, or color is not possible using this method, it involves much

Turnips, ready to be transplanted for seed production.

less work than wintering over the turnips in storage.

The first year's crop can be planted, then thinned to three or four inches apart, in rows spaced two feet apart. Planting time should be calculated based on the expected first frost date for your area (see map, p. 185). Aim for roots that have not quite reached market size when cold weather halts their growth. This means midsummer planting in northern regions and early fall planting further south. Prior to the second year, enough turnips should be harvested to provide 18 inches of space between plants.

During the second year, the seed stalks should be watched carefully, and, when the seedpods have turned yellow, the stalk should be cut, then handled like cabbage stalks (see p. 80).

RUTABAGA (*Brassica napus,* Napobrassica Group). Biennial. Perfect flowers (having both male and female parts). Pollinated by bees.

Rutabaga in its first year of growth.

This vegetable is also commonly known as Swede turnip, and is much like the turnip, except that it is most commonly grown in the northern part of this country, and in the cooler areas of Canada, while turnips are more commonly grown further south. Colors range from buff (the most common) to white, green, and purple.

For growing instructions, see the Turnip entry. The only major difference is that rutabaga must be planted earlier than turnip, since it grows more slowly. When using the seed-to-seed method, sow in early August; for the root-to-seed method, plant in early June.

HORSERADISH *(Armoracia rusticana)*. Perennial.

Horseradish is propagated by planting sections of either the main root or the smaller lateral roots of a parent plant. Those planting it should be absolutely certain they want horseradish growing in that site henceforth, because, once established, horseradish is very difficult to eliminate. Any root left behind in digging will grow again.

In the late fall or early winter, when the root is at its pungent best, dig up the root, cut it into sections four to six inches long, and replant, a foot apart, with the large ends up, as they were growing.

RADISH *(Raphanus sativus)*. Annual. (But the larger Oriental or winter radishes are biennial.) Perfect flowers (having both male and female parts). Cross-pollinated by bees.

The annual radish is that spicy vegetable of which we grow too many in our frantic desire for something quick and in quantity from the garden in the early spring. It will cross easily with other radish varieties, and with others in its group, as explained at the beginning of this section, and so only one variety of the group should be permitted to flower at the same time in the home garden. For professional growers, the minimum isolation distance is one-quarter mile. You may wish to grow extra seed for sprouts for fresh consumption.

A row of white radishes being thinned.

If the beginner has difficulty getting seeds from radish plants, consider these three possible reasons:

1. Bees are required for pollination, and often the small white-to-lilac flower of the radish will not attract bees, if other flowers are available to them.

2. Hot weather. The best-tasting radishes are grown in the cool of the spring. The best crops of seeds are also grown in relatively cool weather, with production cut when periods of temperatures over 90°F. (32°C.) are experienced.

3. Dry weather, too, results in fewer radish seeds, although the radish is more tolerant of dry weather than are the cabbage and its near relatives.

Two methods are used in growing radish seeds:

Root-to-seed. Plant seeds as if growing for the table, thinning them to two inches apart in rows as close as a foot apart. In three or four weeks, depending on the variety of root, the radishes will be large enough to eat. Rogue them, saving the radishes that have the best size, shape, and color, and eating the remainder. Immediately after this roguing, prepare the roots for planting by cutting off all but about one inch of the leaves. Look closely at the top of a radish. You will see small central leaves beginning to develop. Do not cut these.

Replant the radishes, setting the roots in the soil so that the crown of the radish is at ground level. The plants will produce seed stalks two to three feet high, so give them enough room — set the radishes about eight inches apart in rows spaced three feet apart.

The careful gardener will rogue once more, pulling up and discarding those plants that bolt first, since early bolting is not a characteristic to encourage. Careful roguing at this time (and earlier) will do much to maintain the quality of the seed grown.

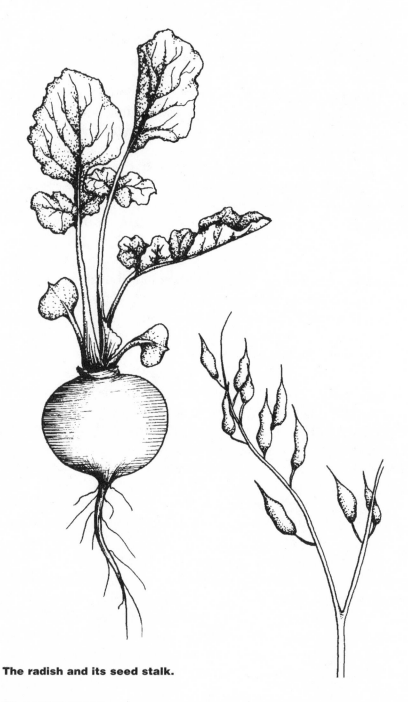

The radish and its seed stalk.

Seed-to-seed. This method saves time and labor, but it results in poorer quality seed, since roguing out the undesirable plants is not as selective as with the first method.

Plant seeds in rows spaced three feet apart, and thin plants to eight or more inches apart. When thinning, rogue out any undesirable plants. You can do a better job of roguing if you pull away enough soil from the top of the roots so that you can see their color. Any that are off-colored should be removed.

In the North, planting in the spring is advised. Further south, the gardener may plant in the fall, and plan on getting a seed stalk growth the following spring.

The radish seeds develop in pods. Unlike cabbage seedpods, though, these pods will not break open when dry, and so the precautions for saving seeds from dehiscent pods need not be taken.

Plants should remain in the garden until most of the pods are brown. You can then open the pods by hand. Dry the pods further if they are difficult to open. The seeds are yellow at first, even when mature, but they will gradually turn to the shade of brown familiar to most gardeners.

The biennial radish, called *daikon* by the Japanese, is unfamiliar to many gardeners who would appreciate both its taste and the ease with which it can be stored to be cooked in the winter. To raise daikon radish seed, follow instructions for Turnip (p. 87).

Fabaceae
BEAN FAMILY

Beginners, here's the perfect starting place if you're interested in growing seeds.

It's hard to go wrong growing peas or beans for seed. You don't need to provide the walled security and isolation of a nunnery in order to defend and preserve their purity. A row of some other crop — preferably a tall one — between rows of different varieties of peas, and 150 feet between different varieties of beans, will prevent crosses.

Peas and beans are annuals, so growing plants need not be carried over from one season to another. And the seeds are large, which makes harvesting them easy. There's another plus to raising these vegetables. If you are careful and industrious enough to mind your peas and beans (and lucky), you can produce a superior variety of either one. You will have vegetables that do best in your garden, because over several generations they have become acclimated to your soil and your growing conditions.

You'll be tempted to grow your usual crops of these two vegetables, and then, when you have picked what you want to eat, let the remainder dry on the vines, saving them for seeds.

DON'T DO IT. You may be saving seed from less-than-desirable plants, and you probably will be saving late-growing seeds, and thus possibly breeding that characteristic into your seeds.

There are many ways to divide your rows between eating and saving for seeds. A recommended method is to mark off 10 or 15 feet of a row for seeds. Put a string around that section. It will remind you and others not to pick from it. Treat this section like royalty. Give it that extra amount of compost. (But not too much fertilizer that's heavy on nitrogen. That will produce lush plants, and fewer seeds.) Carefully rogue out any weak or undesirable plants. Make certain the individual plants have enough elbow room to attain full growth. Weed that plot carefully so the crop does not compete with other plants for food, light, or moisture.

Later, when you have grown, harvested, dried, and packaged your seed, mark the container carefully with the year of growth, and the variety of seeds. Some years ago I planted green beans, and carefully saved a section of a row for seeds. The beans were delicious and the bushes were loaded with them. I'd made a good choice. Suddenly I realized … I'd forgotten what variety I had planted. Now each fall, after I have dried and packaged some of those beans for seed, I mark the container, "Brand X." It's a reminder to me not to make that particular mistake again.

PEA *(Pisum sativum)*. Annual. Self-fertile, but to preserve purity of seed, avoid planting adjacent rows of different varieties.

If you can grow a good crop of peas for eating, you can grow them for seed. Peas do best when planted before the final spring frost, and ideal growing conditions for them are slowly warming days. Peas are planted early: in December and January in the Coastal Plains,

Peas, showing flowers and seedpods.

Gulf Coast regions, and California; in late January and February in the mid-South, and in April and early May in the northernmost areas of the country. Pea plants are hardy enough to live through frosts, although heavy freezing will delay the crop. The gardener who gets the earliest crop of peas gets the best peas, and this is equally true of peas grown for seed.

During the growing season rogue out any weak plants, or plants that are off-color or undesirable in any other way. Plants with small, narrow leaves are commonly found among some varieties, and should be rogued out.

When the peas reach edible size, resist the temptation to harvest them for eating. Wait another month. By now the pods are brown and dry, and the peas inside them are dry enough to rattle when the pods are shaken.

Many commercial growers pull up the plants, then stack or windrow them for further drying. If you have the time, try this method: Pick the pods by pulling up the plants, then stripping off all of the pods. Spread them out under cover, such as in a barn, for further drying. By doing this, you will avoid the possibility of the pods getting rained on, and the damp peas sprouting and becoming worthless as seeds. If well dried, peas can be left in the pods for weeks or even months. Removing them from the pods is a good job for winter, when there isn't as much work to do outside. You should get at least one pound of seed for every 12 feet of row you grow for seed.

There are several methods of removing the seed from the pods. If you harvest one bushel or less, the seeds may be removed by hand. Because the pods are dry, this job can be done quickly and easily.

If you have more than a bushel, try threshing them out. Spread the pods on a blanket or canvas, and beat them with a flail made of two sticks attached by a short piece of leather. Control your enthusiasm as you thresh. Break open the pods, but don't break apart the peas. Since the peas tend to fall to the blanket or canvas surface, most of the trash can be removed quickly with a rake or pitchfork. Then gather the corners of the blanket or canvas to bring the peas

A section of peas, reserved for seed production.

together in a pile, and remove the remainder of the trash by hand.

If dirt and trash remain in the seeds, remove them by taking the seeds outside on a windy day and pouring them from one bowl to another. If you are in doubt about how dry the seeds are after three or more weeks of drying, let them dry for another week or two, well spread out so that moisture is not trapped under layers of seed.

The professional seed grower has moisture computers that will read out the moisture percentage of seeds at the touch of a button. The amateur can't afford this equipment, so it is meaningless to quote desired percentages of moisture to home gardeners. Remember, though, that seed viability depends on low moisture content as well as low temperature, and that maintenance of either at a low level will do much to extend the viability of the seed. Remember, too, that, no matter how dry the seed is at the time of storing, it will soon have the moisture level of the air around it. Thus the emphasis on finding a cool, dry location for storage.

Many people recommend storing peas and beans in airtight containers. I don't. Several attempts at this under varying conditions have resulted in peculiar smells, the growth of fungi, spoilage — and lower viability. I have had no difficulty with placing seeds in burlap bags and storing them under cool, dry conditions out of reach of vermin.

PEANUT *(Arachis hypogaea)*. Annual. Self-pollinated, but avoid adjacent planting of different varieties.

Peanuts, also called groundnuts or goobers, are interesting to grow in the home garden, but require a long, warm growing season for best results. I have raised them from transplants here in the North with some success.

After the bright yellow flowers are pollinated, the fruit stalk elongates and pushes the ovary, or "peg," into the soil. When the leaves begin to turn yellow late in the season, pull up or dig the entire plant. Store for several weeks in a warm, dry place. Remove the fruits from the plant. Store in a cool, dry place. Shell out the seeds before planting. Be careful not to injure the thin papery seed coat while handling the seeds.

BEAN *(Phaseolus vulgaris)*. Annual. Perfect flower (having both male and female parts). Usually self-pollinating before the flower opens, so there is little chance of cross-pollination.

While beans cross-pollinate somewhat more frequently than peas, there is still little opportunity for this, so a row of some vegetable planted between rows of different varieties of beans will decrease even the minimal likelihood of cross-pollination. For greatest protection, plant different varieties 150 feet apart.

All of the beans are grown for seed in the same manner. And all, to some extent, have the same limiting factor when being raised

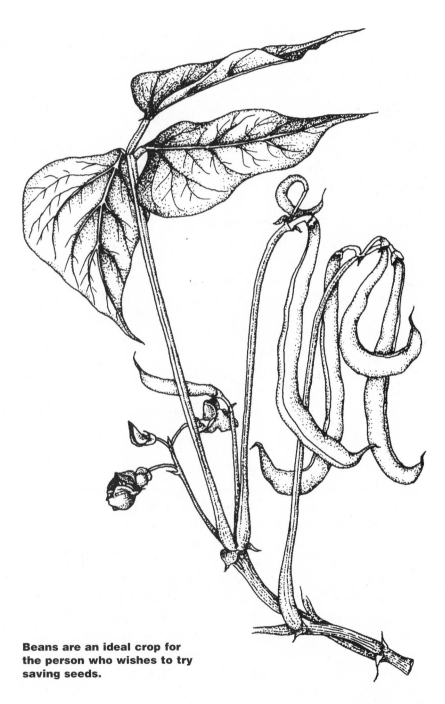

Beans are an ideal crop for the person who wishes to try saving seeds.

for seed. They must be started after all danger of frost is past, and they must be harvested before freezing injures the seed. Thus, many areas of the North simply do not have a long enough growing season for some varieties of beans.

An example is the lima bean. The famous Burpee's Best, a pole lima bean, requires 92 days to reach eating size. Add another six weeks to this for maturity as seeds, and that's a requirement for a 134-day growing season between even light frosts — far too long for most of the northern states and Canada.

If you have grown such dry beans as navy or kidney beans with success, you can, of course, grow these as well as snap beans for seed without worrying about the length of the growing season.

When growing these beans for seed, grow them as you would a crop for eating, but rogue out any plants with undesirable qualities. Beans are planted after all danger of frost is past, but will react to weather in other ways, as well. They will drop blossoms during a heat wave, for instance, and fail to produce if the weather turns cool and rainy.

Plant bush beans in rows spaced two feet apart, with plants thinned to four inches apart. Pole bean rows should be spaced at least three feet apart.

Be on the lookout for the various seed-borne diseases listed in the table on p. 137. Anthracnose is especially common.

The harvesting time for seeds can be estimated by watching the crop reach the harvesting size for eating, with the pods nearly full-grown and the beans not yet fully developed. The beans should be ready for harvesting as seeds about six weeks later, or when most of the pods have turned brown.

The person who is harvesting only one or two bushels may find it easy to pick the beans, spread them out (indoors, if you have rainy autumns) to cure for a week or two, then shell them.

For larger amounts, pull up the plants, let them dry in piles or windrows for one or two weeks, until brittle, then flail them. If rain is predicted during the drying period, try to dry them indoors.

In flailing, most of the trash can be removed with a pitchfork or rake, with the remainder removed by winnowing.

Seeds should be stored in a cool, dry place — not in airtight containers.

LIMA BEAN *(Phaseolus lunatus)* can't be grown for eating in the green stage in many of the northern regions. Ideally limas should have two months of above 50°F. (10°C.) night temperatures, with planting delayed until the soil is warm. Add six more weeks of frost-free weather at the end of this two-month period for growing these

Lima beans, not yet ready to be picked for seeds.

beans for seed, and the reason they can't be grown in the North for seed becomes obvious.

Both bush and pole varieties of lima beans are available. All the steps of growing, harvesting, drying, and storage are the same as for other beans. Limas can be easily damaged during and after harvest, so care should be taken with them.

COWPEA *(Vigna unguiculata)* is grown in the South (where it is often called a *southern pea* or a *field pea:* the green pea of the rest of the nation is an *English pea*) and in California (where it is called a *black-eyed pea)*. Many families in the South save this seed each year, proud of the taste qualities of the strain they nurture.

This warm-weather crop is grown much like lima beans, with planting delayed until the soil is warm, when seed is planted three inches apart, in rows spaced 30 to 36 inches apart.

Follow instructions under Beans for harvesting, drying, and storage.

SOYBEAN *(Glycine max)*. This is a crop of growing interest to the home gardener, because of the many uses and the high protein content of the soybean, with the larger-seeded garden varieties the choice to grow.

Like lima beans, most of the soybeans can be planted only when the soil is warm, and most have a long growing season. However, several seed companies in northern areas have worked on, and now offer for sale, soybeans with growing seasons short enough to be grown in most areas of the United States.

Follow instructions under Beans for harvesting, drying, and storage.

Malvaceae
MALLOW FAMILY

This family includes familiar flowers, such as the hollyhock (see p. 153), an important commercial plant, cotton, a few trees and weeds — and one garden vegetable, okra.

OKRA *(Abelmoschus esculentus)*. Annual. Self-pollinating. Some cross-pollination may occur within one mile.

This plant produces a yellow flower with a red center followed within several days by a pod, which is harvested for eating before it has become fully developed.

For seeds, pods should be left on the plants to become woody, and with the seeds fully developed. Harvest pods in late fall, crack them open, and remove the seeds.

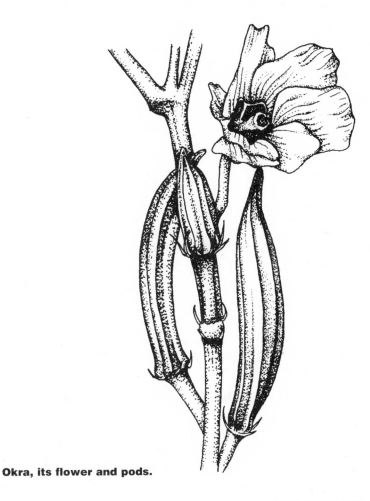

Okra, its flower and pods.

Apiaceae
Celery Family

The gardener who wishes to grow seeds of biennials is encouraged to select from this group. Carrying the plants over to the second year of growth is not a major problem with these vegetables as it can be, for example, with the members of the Mustard Family. The major problem for home growers is that the different varieties of each plant will cross unless separated by long distances, and the garden carrot will cross with its wild and prolific relative, Queen Anne's lace.

Most of the seeds in this family have low viability, so they should be tested before planting. All of them flower and form seed in the second year of growth.

CARROT (*Daucus carota* var. *sativa*). Biennial. Perfect flowers (having both male and female parts). Pollinated by insects.

There are two methods of growing carrot seed:

Root-to-seed, the recommended method. In the first year, plant seed late enough in the spring so that the plant reaches maturity in late fall. The carrots can be dug up any time before the ground freezes. Cut the tops off, taking care not to cut into the growing point of the plant's crown. Leave about an inch of growth.

Rogue out the crop at this time, reserving for table use any carrots that are misshapen, off-color, small, cracked, or damaged during harvesting.

In mild climates, the carrots can be replanted immediately after this roguing. In cooler areas, replanting in the late fall is possible, too, with a heavy mulch giving the roots more than adequate protection. Or the roots can be stored for spring planting.

Near-freezing temperatures and high humidity are ideal for

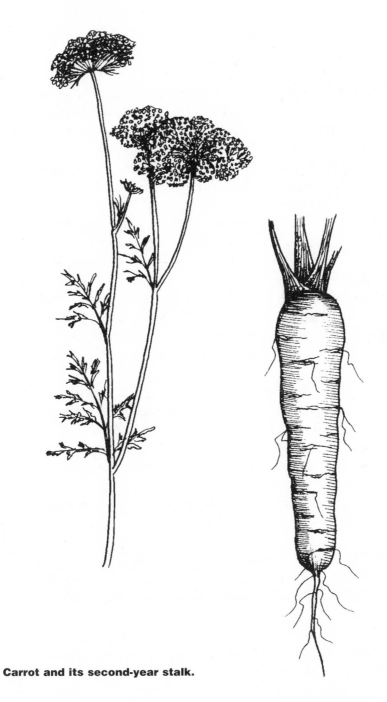

Carrot and its second-year stalk.

storage. These conditions will generally be found in a root or cold cellar. For further protection, carrots can be stored in boxes of damp sand or sawdust.

In the spring, when the soil can be worked, check over the stored carrots and discard any that have shriveled or decayed. The carrots should not be left to dry out before replanting, but should be set out quickly in moist soil. If the soil tends to be dry, soak each carrot after it is planted. Replant the carrots one foot apart, in rows spaced three feet apart, with the carrot's crown set at or just below the surface level of the soil.

There are two common methods for setting out the carrots. The first is to insert a shovel into the soil, then push it forward, and plant a carrot in the space. Make sure you firm up the soil around each carrot as it is planted.

The second method is to rototill the soil, then simply press the carrot down into the loosened soil, making sure that the root is planted deep enough so that the crown is at the surface level of the soil when the soil has been packed around it.

Seed-to-seed is the other method of growing carrots for seed, and it involves leaving the carrot in place for two seasons. This method requires less work than the root-to-seed procedure, but has certain disadvantages. For one thing, the grower cannot rogue out undesirable roots, so the quality of seeds may deteriorate gradually. Carrying carrots through the winter, too, can be troublesome. Alternate freezing and thawing may thrust the roots up out of the ground (a problem that can usually be avoided by mulching them). Finally, the gardener may tend to crowd the crop using this method, leaving too many carrots in the row during the first growing season, and not reducing the number of carrots to space plants one foot apart in rows three feet apart in the second year of growth.

No matter which method is used, the soil should be loose and high in organic matter, and should never be permitted to dry out. Weed the carrot patch carefully to provide ideal growing conditions.

Carrots being harvested for storage.

Commercial growers separate different carrot varieties by a minimum of one mile. Your alternative is to carry only one variety at a time into the second year of growth, although other varieties can, of course, be grown for first-year harvesting. Check your area for Queen Anne's lace, and make certain it is cut back and not in bloom when your carrots blossom in the second year.

If you've grown carrots only as annuals for eating, you'll be surprised at that second year's growth — two to six feet high, with a fairly large head, and a series of branches beneath it. Flowers will appear first on the head, then on the top branches, and finally on the lower branches. This is also the order in which the seeds develop and mature. The seeds are ready for harvesting when the heads of the top branches have turned brown. This will be in September in most areas. They will not shatter easily, so exact timing of harvesting isn't necessary.

For harvesting a small crop, pull up the entire plant, and form

Queen Anne's lace, the flowering weed, looks much like the second-year growth of carrots.

small piles of them. They should be cured until the stalks snap when bent. This may take two or three weeks in moist climates. You can speed up this process by placing the plants under cover to cure.

Another method of harvesting is to cut off the heads as they mature (turn brown), and take them indoors to dry.

Rub the seed heads together to free the seed. The quickest way to remove stems and other unwanted material from the seed is to build a screen that will permit seeds to fall through but will sort out the other debris.

The carrot seeds you retrieve will have small spines. Commercial growers remove these so that the seed can be used in mechanical seeders. If you wish to remove them, rub the seeds briskly between your hands.

CELERIAC *(Apium graveolens* var. *rapaceum).* Biennial. Perfect flowers (having both male and female parts). Cross-pollinated by insects.

This vegetable, unfamiliar to many gardeners, is grown for its roots. While it is closely related to celery, the methods used to grow seed are very similar to those for carrots.

Celery and celeriac will cross, so only one of these should be grown a second year for seed in any season.

In the second year, the plants should be watched carefully, since all of the seeds will not mature at the same time, and the seed tends to shatter. You can save this early seed by holding the browned heads in a paper bag and shaking them.

Follow instructions under the Carrot entry for growing, harvesting, and drying the seeds.

CELERY *(Apium graveolens* var. *dulce)*. Biennial. Perfect flowers (having both male and female parts). Cross-pollinated by insects.

This is probably the most difficult of the plants in this family to raise for seed, because of the greater difficulty in wintering over the plants.

In the North, because of celery's long growing season, this vegetable must be started indoors or in a cold frame, then transplanted outdoors. This is not necessary in the areas of milder weather that provide the 115- to 135-day growing season this crop requires.

In the fall, select the best plants for seed. They should be dug up, roots intact, then placed in a cold cellar, with the roots in soil and the vegetation blanketed in straw. Near-freezing temperatures and high humidity are required.

After the danger of frost is past in the spring, uncover the plants, remove the rotted leaves and stalks, and replant, two feet apart, in rows spaced three feet apart.

In warm areas such as California and the South, the timing is changed by sowing in July, then transplanting the plants in January.

This avoids the need to store the plants.

The second-year growth is two to three feet high and extremely bushy. Tiny white flowers appear first on the top of the plant, then bloom on the lower branches. Seeds will turn brown and become ready for harvesting in this same order. Since many seeds can be lost through shattering, you should try to save the earlier seeds by shaking the top heads into a paper bag.

Follow the directions for harvesting given for carrots. Dry heads on a canvas, so that seeds that fall will not be lost.

Remember that celery and celeriac will cross with each other, so plan to have only one of these blossoming in any one season.

PARSLEY *(Petroselinum crispum)*. Biennial. Perfect flowers (having both male and female parts). Pollinated by insects.

Parsley seeds, even under ideal conditions, do not retain their viability for more than one to two years. New seed should be harvested every year.

Parsley seeds, slow to germinate, may be speeded along by soaking them overnight the night before planting. They can be started indoors or in cold frames, then transplanted to the garden, set out one foot apart.

In the fall, select the most desirable plants, and transplant them to where you wish them to grow by digging them up with a spadeful of soil. Set them two feet apart in rows spaced two feet apart. After the first few heavy frosts, cover them with a mulch of leaves or hay. They will survive well, even in northern areas.

Uncover them as growth starts in the spring. They will grow to two or more feet in height, with many branches and small flower heads. Seeds are ready for harvesting when they turn brown, in September in most areas. The seeds will shatter, so you should collect the first seeds that mature by shaking the heads inside a paper bag. When most of the heads have turned brown, cut them off and let them cure indoors on canvas or papers so any seeds that fall will not be lost.

Clean and process parsley seeds like carrot seeds (though parsley seeds do not have spines).

PARSNIP *(Pastinaca sativa)*. Biennial. Perfect flowers (having both male and female parts). Pollinated by insects.

Parsnip seeds lose viability in one or two years, so fresh seed should be grown each year. This is the slowest-growing member of this family.

Parsnips can be grown using either the seed-to-seed or root-to-seed method, as described in the Carrot entry (see p. 104). You will probably be tempted to use the former method, because, even in the coldest climates, parsnips will winter over without difficulty.

For superior seed, however, you should use the root-to-seed method, digging up the parsnips in the early spring, when they are ordinarily dug up for eating, then replanting them three feet apart in rows spaced three feet apart, with the crowns at soil level. For the best seed, select the best of the roots for replanting, and dine on the remainder. You can, of course, dig up the roots in the fall, store them as you would carrots, then replant them in the spring.

The second-year plant will send up a bushy seed stalk, three to four feet in height. The yellowish flowers are followed by the brown seeds in the fall. Harvest as for carrot seed. Since parsnip seeds shatter, shake the early heads into a paper bag to avoid loss.

Parsnip will cross with the true wild parsnip *(Pastinaca sativa* var. *sylvestris)*, the root of which has a strong parsnip aroma.

Solanaceae
NIGHTSHADE FAMILY

This family includes the eggplant, pepper, potato, and tomato. Most growers of seed will want to try one of these, probably the tomato. Again, don't try to save seed from the hybrid varieties. It won't work.

(And if you *do* try it, as you will if you are the curious type, expect some seed that won't germinate, plus plants that lack the uniformity and vigor of their parents — and that may not even resemble them, since the tendency is for them to revert one of the types of plants used to create the hybrid.)

For each of these vegetables there are open-pollinated varieties with admirable qualities, and seeds that will not give you unpleasant surprises. For the names and descriptions of nonhybrid varieties, consult the *Garden Seed Inventory,* published by Seed Savers Exchange of Decorah, Iowa (for information, see p. 171).

EGGPLANT *(Solanum melongena* var. *esculentum).* Annual. Perfect flowers (having both male and female parts). Self-pollinated, but crossing will occur, since flowers sometimes attract insects.

Eggplant likes a growing season that is both long and warm. However, by starting plants indoors or in cold frames, and setting them out when the soil has warmed up, gardeners in all but the coldest parts of the country can raise eggplant.

While cross-pollination is not a major problem, you can avoid any possibility of this if you raise only one variety during a season when you expect to save seed.

Identify and save for seed the best fruits on several of your best plants. The remaining plants can produce eggplants for eating, after any with undesirable traits have been rogued out.

If possible, leave the fruit on the plant until it falls off, which is an indication that the seeds are mature. If frosts threaten, and the fruit is ripe enough for eating, pick it and take it indoors. In about two weeks (don't wait until it is rotting) the fruit will produce mature seeds.

Cut the fruit and remove the placenta, or the seed-bearing portion. Place this in a container (a glass bowl works fine), add water, and work the mass with your fingers. Gradually the seeds will separate and sink to the bottom, and the remaining material and

The eggplant, its blossom and its fruit.

Here's an eggplant selected for seed production.

water can be poured off. Several washings may be necessary.

Spread out the seeds on paper towels or screens, and dry them thoroughly. If, after drying, the seeds stick together, rub them together gently in your hands to separate them.

PEPPER *(Capsicum annuum)*. Annual, but perennial in tropical areas. Perfect flowers (having both male and female parts). Self-pollinated, but some crossing can be expected if different varieties are planted in adjacent rows, due to bee activity.

Grow plants in the same way as you would for a food crop. Rogue out any undesirable plants, to avoid cross-pollination with better plants. Select and identify excellent fruits on several of your best plants. Let these ripen far beyond the stage at which you would ordinarily pick them for eating. The peppers are ready for seed production when they have turned color and have begun to shrivel. If your growing season does not permit them to ripen that far, pick the peppers and take them indoors to ripen further.

Cut open the peppers and remove the seeds. If this is done carefully, there should be little or no unwanted material mixed in with the seeds. Dry the seeds thoroughly and store.

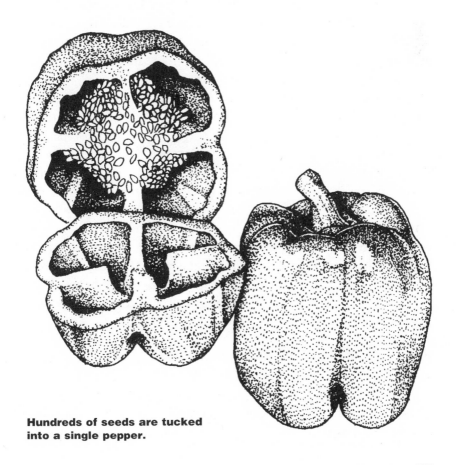

Hundreds of seeds are tucked into a single pepper.

TOMATO *(Lycopersicon lycopersicum)*. Annual, although it's a perennial in its native South America. Perfect flowers (having both male and female parts). Self-pollinated, although some crossing may occur from bee activity.

If you have been growing hybrid tomatoes, but would like to grow the nonhybrid varieties for seed as well as for eating, try several varieties the first year. In this way you can most quickly find the variety or varieties that best meet your needs. Plant at least three plants of each variety, separating the varieties by as much garden space as possible.

Tomatoes are tropical plants, and do best in long, hot growing seasons. Those of us who live in cooler areas know the race we watch each summer, wondering whether the peak of the tomato season will beat the first killing frost. In areas such as these, many seed growers strive for early producers.

Identify and mark several of the best and earliest plants of each variety. Let the fruit reach full ripeness, then pick the best of them from those plants. Cut them open and scoop out the seeds and pulp, mixing seeds and pulp from several plants, but of course keeping the different varieties separate. Place the mixture in glass jars, with a jar for each variety, and add a small amount of water. Stir two or three times daily. The fermentation that results helps separate the seeds from the other materials. Depending on the room temperature, the seeds will separate and sink to the bottom of the jar in from two (warm room) to four days. Add more water, then pour off the pulp, repeating this procedure until the seeds are clean.

Spread the seeds out on paper towels or screens to dry.

POTATO *(Solanum tuberosum)*. Annual. Self-pollinated.

The true seed of the potato is used mostly in breeding programs. The tuber (that's the potato) is used for propagation as well as for eating. Tubers grown specifically for propagation are often called seed potatoes.

**The perfect flowers and tiny, immature
fruit of the tomato plant.**

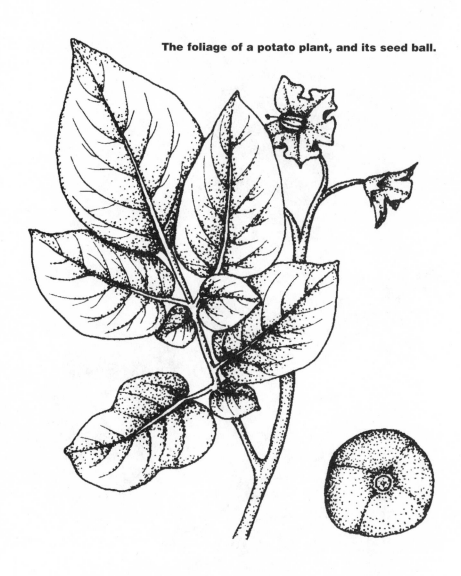

The foliage of a potato plant, and its seed ball.

If you want to raise potatoes for both eating and propagation, start with certified disease-free potatoes. Mark the plants that are healthiest and most disease-free, and take your seed potatoes from them. Discard any tubers with discolored flesh or soft spots on their skin. I have tried planting with both the small and the large potatoes from these plants, and see no difference. It is logical, then, to eat the larger potatoes and save the smaller ones to start the next season's crop.

Potatoes, of course, have been and are grown from seed. A famous example is that of the Burbank potato, which was one of 23 otherwise worthless seedlings grown by Luther Burbank from seed saved from a single potato seed ball.

You may not find many seed balls in your patch of highly selected, civilized potatoes, but if you do come across a potato plant that bears seed (the seed ball resembles a tiny green tomato), and you want to experiment, save the seed for planting early the next spring. Just don't count on it for your whole crop of potatoes.

Cucurbitaceae
GOURD OR CUCUMBER FAMILY

If you've been successful raising peas or beans for seed, and now want to try your hand at something slightly more complicated, here is your next move. This family includes the cucumber, gourd, squash, pumpkin, muskmelon (including cantaloupe), and watermelon.

You've probably raised some or all of these vegetables for eating. Pick one that you feel confident growing, and raise it for seeds. Remember to follow the rules to avoid unwanted crosses between these vegetables. This is a case where failures often produce most startling results.

First, a few general rules:

1. Don't worry about crosses between any combination of cucumbers, squashes, and melons. They won't happen. You won't raise any squamelons or melocumbers, despite what some old gardener may tell you. The so-called Melon Squash is a variety of *Cucurbita moschata*.

2. Crosses *will* occur between varieties of each vegetable. Thus, two varieties of cucumbers will cross, and this is undesirable if you are saving seed.

3. Don't worry about crosses if you are growing crops to eat, not for seed. The female, or pistillate, blossoms will dominate, so all of the acorn squash (for example) on a single plant will be the same for eating purposes, even though some of the blossoms were pollinated from male acorn squash blossoms, and others from male zucchini squash blossoms.

Let's start out with a discussion of squash and pumpkins, since this is where much of the confusion begins for the seed grower. There are just a few simple rules to learn; then you'll feel that superiority that can come when you understand what few others have mastered.

SQUASH *(Cucurbita* spp.*).* Annual. Monoecious (having separate male and female blossoms on the same plant). Cross-pollinated, usually by bees.

What about crosses between pumpkins and squash? Is there any easy-to-learn rule that just can't be forgotten? Unfortunately, no. They don't divide simply and logically, such as all winter squash in one group, all summer squash in another, and pumpkins in a third.

Instead, there are four species (you may find only three listed in older references), and here are their easily recognized characteristics, and the best-known varieties of each species:

Cucurbita maxima. Vines 15 to 20 feet long. Huge leaves. Stem is soft, round, and hairy. Long growing season. The numerous varieties include Buttercup, Hubbard, Delicious, and Hokkiado.

Cucurbita moschata. Large leaves and spreading vines. The

smooth, five-sided corky stem flares out as it joins the fruit. Butternut is the classic and most common example of this species. (A new Butternut bush variety lacks the characteristic spreading vines.)

Cucurbita pepo. Both bush and long-vined. Stem is five-sided. Branches, too, have five sides, and spines. All of the familiar summer squash fall into this species, including Zucchini, Yellow Crookneck, Vegetable Spaghetti, Acorn, Lady Godiva, White Bush Scallop, Cocozelle, and the common pumpkin.

Cucurbita mixta. This species formerly was lumped with *Cucurbita moschata,* and has similar characteristics. The most familiar variety is the Green-Striped Cushaw.

The varieties within each species *will* cross. And research has shown that there is also some crossing *between* varieties of different species, specifically:

C. *pepo* and C. *moschata.*
C. *pepo* and C. *mixta.*
C. *moschata* and C. *maxima.*

In your home garden, do not raise more than one variety from each species. In a large planting, a distance of 500 feet is usually enough to prevent crossing. Separate as far as possible varieties of different species if there is some chance of crossing, as indicated in the previous paragraph.

If you wish to raise two or more varieties of a particular species, or if your over-the-fence neighbor raises them, there is a method you can use to insure the purity of the seed you harvest. It's hand-pollinating.

This procedure involves protecting the female blossom both before and after hand-pollinating, and protecting the male blossom until it has been used for pollination.

Male and female blossoms from the same plant can be used,

since the squashes do not lose vigor when inbred in this way.

Before you begin, you must learn two things: how to tell a male from a female blossom, and how to find buds that will open the following day.

Identifying the male and female blossoms is simple. The female bud has the beginning of the squash — a miniature fruit that is really an ovary — at its base, while the stem of the male buds leads directly into the bud.

The blossoms that will open the following day are those that have a definite orange color, rather than only green.

Select six or so female buds for your first effort, identifying them on a sunny afternoon. Place a paper bag over each one, marking an "F" on the bag so that it will be plain to you the following day that this is one of the female buds. The nonplastic bags used by supermarkets for pints of ice cream are ideal for this work, since they are heavy and thus will endure the dews and even the rains of several days. Tie (but not tightly over the stem), staple (but not through the stem), or paper-clip the bag in place, close enough so that no exploring honeybee will find her way into it. Protect an equal number of male buds. The same type of bags can be used, or, because the bud needs to be held closed only overnight, you can simply slip a rubber band over the end of the bud, holding it shut. In the past, I have tried using twine, and it worked fine, although tying it without damaging the bud was more of a problem.

On the following morning, pick one of the male blossoms that you have fastened shut with a rubber band. Carry it to one of the covered female blossoms. Uncover the female blossom, and remove its petals. Take the rubber band off the male blossom and remove its petals. You will see the stamen and its pollen. Gently rub this stamen against the stigma of the female blossom so that the pollen clings to the stigma. Discard the male blossom, and cover the female blossom again with the paper bag. Leave it in place for about four days. After removing the bag, mark the stem of the female blossom in some way so that the right squash can be found at harvesting time. A bright ribbon tied loosely around the stem is one way to do this.

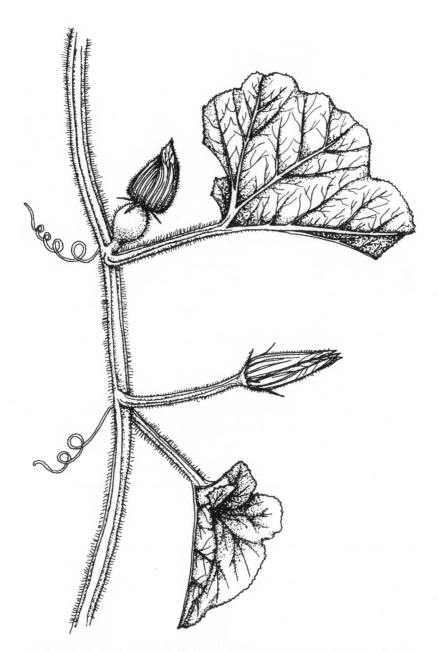

This drawing shows the difference between the female bud, with the round ball called an ovary, and the male, with its longer, thin stem.

Look for the rounded ovary at the base of the female bud (left) to differentiate it from the male blossom (right).

Repeat this process for each female blossom. This is one of those simple procedures that can be done much more quickly than it can be described, so don't be talked out of trying it by the detail given here.

The squash and pumpkin plants should be watched during all periods of growth, so that any with undesirable traits can be rogued out.

The seed of the winter varieties and pumpkins is mature when the squash or pumpkin is mature and ready for harvesting in the fall. The summer squash, however, must grow far beyond the harvesting stage, until it has reached full growth and has hardened. If you have raised zucchini squash, and one hid under the heavy foliage and grew to a huge size, you have grown zucchini to the proper size for seed.

Squash for seed should be harvested in the fall, at about the time of the first frost. Because the squash will keep for many months, there is no urgency about removing the seeds. It's a good job for the early winter. Cut the squash in two, but avoid slicing through the central seed cavity. The seeds and the moist material around them can be removed with a large kitchen spoon. Place all of this material in a large bowl, add some water, and work the mixture through your fingers. The seeds will separate gradually. Wash them again, then spread them out on paper or screens to dry. Give them up to a week of drying, moving them about daily so that they do not remain in small, wet piles, retaining the moisture.

Once dry, the seeds can be kept in a sealed jar. It's a good idea to check them two or three weeks after placing them in the jar. If there is any sign of moisture, spread the seeds out again for further drying. After all the trouble you've gone to, this is not the time to take a chance on spoilage.

This fruit is clearly identified for saving.

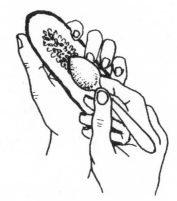

The four easy steps for saving cucumber seed. First, split the cucumber lengthwise, then, using a spoon, scrape out all of the seeds and the pulp surrounding them.

As always, be sure to label the container with the variety of seeds and the year of growing. You may remember — and then again, you may not.

PUMPKIN. All directions for squash apply to pumpkin.

CUCUMBER *(Cucumis sativus).* Annual. Monoecious (having separate male and female blossoms on the same plant). Cross-pollinated by bees.

Cucumbers will not cross with melons or squashes, but will cross with other varieties of cucumbers. The home gardener thus may grow any other vegetables in the garden, and still raise cucumbers for seed, provided that he or she raises only one variety of cucumber. Because bees pollinate the cucumber blossoms, commercial seed growers strive for a distance of at least a mile between varieties. The home gardener should be concerned about any other varieties within one-quarter mile, but will probably get an undesired cross

Place the mixture in a bowl to ferment. Stir several times daily to keep mold from forming. The pulp will become watery, and the seeds you'll want to save will sink to the bottom. Dry the seeds on a screen.

only if a neighboring garden is growing a different variety. Some method of cooperation, such as growing the same variety, can usually be worked out with the neighbors.

The length of the growing season may be a problem for some gardeners in cold climates. Cucumbers for eating can be raised in 60 to 70 days, with planting started after all danger of frost is past. But the growing season for seeds must be at least five weeks longer to produce the ripe, yellow cucumbers that will have mature seed.

The careful gardener will watch the growth of the cucumber plants through all stages of development, and rogue out any that are not strong and healthy, or that show any undesirable characteristics.

If there is any danger of undesirable crosses, cucumbers can be hand-pollinated, using the system described under Squash.

It's easy to tell the male from the female blossoms. Each plant will have both. The female, or pistillate, flowers are not in groups, as are the male, or staminate, flowers. Beneath the female flower, there is a tiny growth that looks like a small cucumber. This is the ovary.

If you have raised cucumbers, you probably know that there are white-spined varieties, grown for slicing, and black-spined varieties, grown for pickling. The former will be a yellowish-white when mature, while the latter will be much darker, from golden to brown. Any cucumber that does not follow this rule should not be saved for seed.

I have found that cucumber vines are blackened by the first fall frost, and that this makes the selection of cucumbers to be saved for seed an easy task, since suddenly all of the cucumbers are very visible, no longer hidden beneath the green leaves. I select half a dozen cucumbers from as many plants and mix the seeds of all together, even though this gives me far more seeds than I need. If you have hand-pollinated and marked certain cucumbers, these of course will be the ones you use for seed.

Split the cucumber lengthwise, then scrape out the seeds and the pulp surrounding them. A spoon will do the job. Dump this mixture into a large glass bowl, then let it sit and ferment in the kitchen for about five days, stirring it at least once a day to discourage any mold from forming.

By the end of the five days, most of the seed will have separated from the pulp and will be down at the bottom of the bowl. Retrieve several of the seeds and rub them between your fingers. You should discover that their slippery coating has been lost in the fermentation process.

The top layer of pulp and undeveloped seeds can now be removed, leaving the good seeds at the bottom of the bowl. These can be washed by filling the bowl with water (not hot water), letting the seeds settle to the bottom of the bowl, then pouring off the water.

Spread the seeds on paper towels or a screen, separate them as much as possible, then let them dry, either inside or out in the sun. Shake them around occasionally, so that they do not cling together and thus retain moisture.

MUSKMELON (*Cucumis melo,* Reticulatus Group). Annual. Monoecious (having separate male and female blossoms on the same plant). Cross-pollinated by bees.

Growing muskmelons for seed follows most of the instructions for

Muskmelon and its vine.

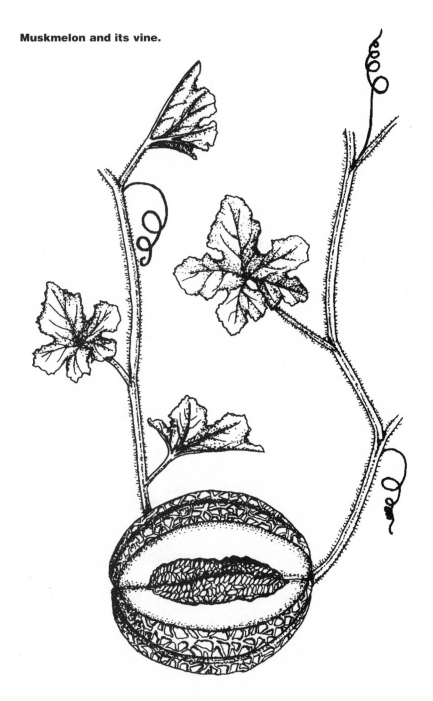

growing cucumbers. There are two major differences:

1. The muskmelon likes warm weather, even more than does the cucumber, and may demand a longer growing season.

2. When the muskmelon is ready to eat, the seeds are mature. This of course means that the melon can be eaten and enjoyed after the seeds and pulp have been removed.

Follow the instructions under Cucumber for isolation, roguing, seed production and harvesting, and for separating seeds from the pulp.

WATERMELON *(Citrullus lanatus).* Annual. Monoecious (having separate male and female blossoms on the same plant). Cross-pollinated by bees.

This melon is grown only in the warmer areas of the country, although the growing area has pushed northward with the development of new, hardier varieties and the use of greenhouses to start plants. The watermelon will cross with citron fruit and other varieties of watermelon, but not with muskmelons, cucumbers, squashes, or pumpkins. The ideal isolation distance is a minimum of one-quarter mile. Watermelon can be pollinated by hand, as described under Squash.

As with muskmelons, the seeds of watermelons are mature when the melon is ready to be eaten. There are several methods that can be used to determine this. One is to check under the watermelon, where it rests on the soil; if this area has turned from white to yellow, the melon should be ripe.

Extracting seeds from watermelon should be a pleasant family effort. The larger the group of participants, the better. Provide several chilled watermelons, cups or bowls for the black seeds, and trash containers or compost buckets for the rinds. Serve slices of watermelon until everyone feels sated, or until the desired number of seeds has been obtained. The fastidious will wash these seeds. In any case, be sure to dry them well.

For other instructions on growing watermelon seeds, see the Cucumber entry.

Asteraceae
ASTER FAMILY

LETTUCE *(Lactuca sativa).* Annual. Perfect flowers (having both male and female parts). Self-pollinated.

Because lettuce is self-pollinating, different varieties can be grown in adjacent rows, although to prevent the occasional crossing, it is better to plant another crop between rows of separate varieties.

You probably think of lettuce as an early crop, but, in growing it for seed, it's a long-season crop.

There are several methods of planting. One is to plant as soon as the soil can be worked, since a frost will not kill the tiny lettuce plants.

Another is to start the seeds indoors, or in a cold frame, then set out the plants about one foot apart. This is an excellent idea for any gardener, assuring one of lettuce to eat at least a month earlier than when the lettuce seed is planted outdoors.

In warmer areas, lettuce is planted in the late fall, and produces seed in the spring.

This same method can be tried in cooler climates for the crisphead varieties that are slow to bolt and produce seeds. The time of late summer planting will vary geographically, but the gardener should aim for plants about two inches in height when cold weather halts growth. This height has proven to be the level at which

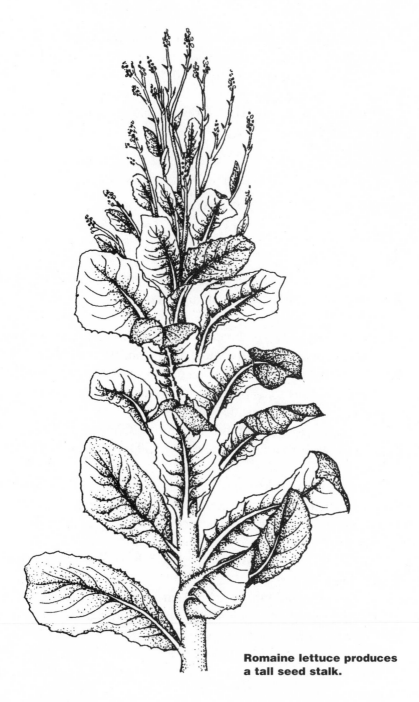

Romaine lettuce produces
a tall seed stalk.

the least winter damage can be expected. The tiny plants can be mulched after the first heavy frost to provide protection. The soil in which they are growing should be well drained. If you try this method, delay thinning the plants until spring.

Aim for a foot of space between plants when the lettuce reaches the bolting stage. If planting is heavier than this, the gardener can remove any plants with undesirable characteristics while thinning.

You should remember that early bolting is not a desirable characteristic, so any plants that bolt and produce seed at a record pace should be pulled and the seeds discarded.

The plants will put up seed stems that are from two to five feet high, with the height depending on the variety.

Some varieties of lettuce, particularly the crispheads, should be encouraged to produce seed stalks by cutting an X into the top of the head as soon as it reaches full growth, or by cutting off the top half of the head, or by opening the leaves at the top of the head. This should not be delayed, since the reason for doing this is to clear the way for the growth of the stem before it begins its growth, rather than after normal development has been halted by the closely packed head.

Lettuce does not produce seed in a way most convenient for the gardener. The yellow flowers open over a period of a month, and the seeds, presenting a feathery appearance on the branches of the seed stalk, mature over a similar period, about 12 days after flowering. If ignored, this early seed will be lost. Shake the plant into a paper bag any time you observe maturing seed. This will provide more and cleaner seeds. Another method is to wait for the branches to have a feathery appearance, then cut them. Dry them for several days on a canvas to save any seed that falls, then shake out the remaining seed. Winnow the seed to remove any trash.

Many varieties of lettuce have been produced that do best in the growing conditions of specific areas. The gardener who starts with a preferred variety of lettuce, who provides good growing conditions, and who discards any undesirable plants, can improve that variety to produce the plants best suited for that garden.

JERUSALEM ARTICHOKE *(Helianthus tuberosus)*. Perennial. Propagated by tubers.

If you have read anything about Jerusalem artichokes, you know that the name is a corruption of words, and that the plant has nothing to do with either Jerusalem or artichokes. It was cultivated by North American Indians, and was a source of pleasure to the empty stomachs of many an early colonist.

Plant tubers four inches deep, two feet apart in rows spaced three feet apart, and in an area of the garden where the plant, all six to eight feet of it, will not shade other crops, and where its missionary zeal toward taking over the entire garden can be curbed. The tubers do not store well after being dug, so they should be left in the ground and dug up in the fall or early spring, as they are needed for eating or for propagation. This tuber is an excellent vegetable, flavorful and crammed with nutrition. It's easy to grow too; neither pest nor disease has challenged the long line of my Jerusalem artichokes, nor slowed its expanding width.

SALSIFY *(Tragopogon porrifolius)*. Biennial. Perfect flowers (having both male and female parts). Self-pollinated.

Salsify is a delicious root vegetable that has won little popularity. Like parsnip, its taste is improved by cold weather. Even in northern Vermont, the roots can be left in the ground during the winter, then dug up for eating in the spring.

If you wish to raise salsify seed, you will carry this process one step further, selecting the best of your roots in the spring and replanting them a foot apart, in rows spaced three feet apart. If you decide not to rogue the plants, simply thin to one root every foot as you are harvesting the rest.

In the second year, the salsify plant will grow to about three feet in height with large, purple flowers. When the seeds develop and mature (with the "feathers" of dandelions), pick the individual

A Jerusalem artichoke blossom.

heads in the morning, and dry them for several days. Then rub the heads between your hands to free the seeds, and winnow them.

TABLE II

A Checklist of Some Seed-Borne Vegetable Diseases

BEAN	Anthracnose (false rust), bacterial blight, bacterial wilt, common mosaic, halo blight
BRASSICAS	Bacterial leaf spot, black leg, black rot
CARROT	Alternaria blight, bacterial blight, early blight
CELERY	Early blight, late blight
CORN	Bacterial blight (Stewart's disease), seedling blight
CUCURBITS	Anthracnose, alternaria blight, angular leaf spot, fusarium wilt, mosaic
EGGPLANT	Fruit rot (phomopsis blight)
LETTUCE	Anthracnose, mosaic, septoria leaf spot
PEA	Ascochyta pod spot, bacterial blight, scab
PEPPER	Anthracnose, bacterial spot, cercospora leaf spot
POTATO *(tubers)*	Bacterial ring spot, black scurf, early blight, late blight, leaf roll, mosaic, scab, wilt
RADISH	Leaf spot
SPINACH	Anthracnose
TOMATO	Bacterial canker, bacterial spot, early blight, nailhead spot, wilt

Many authorities recommend hot water treatment of infected seed: immerse at 125°F. (52°C.) for 15 to 30 minutes just prior to planting. Cool seeds quickly. Alternatively, a 90-second soak in diluted bleach (one part household bleach to nine parts water) followed by a pure water rinse will disinfect the seed coat.

TABLE II **137**

Seed treatment with Captan (or an equivalent fungicide) is practiced commercially and by some home seed savers to control some seed-borne diseases and damping-off. Some agricultural uses of Captan have recently been restricted by the United States Environmental Protection Agency (EPA). Studies have shown that Captan can be carcinogenic or mutagenic in some animals.

Captan is the active ingredient in several household pesticides. In general, its use cannot be encouraged for home gardeners; if you decide to use it anyway, be sure to read the label directions carefully and follow them explicitly.

PART III

The Flowers

The Best Flowering Ornamentals to Save for Seed

Included in this section are common annual and biennial ornamentals that, with varying degrees of effort, can be saved by the home gardener. There are many closely related perennial species, often with names similar to the annuals, that can also be grown from seeds. Perennials, however, are ordinarily propagated vegetatively to maintain varietal distinctions. For information on the various methods of vegetative propagation, refer to Lewis Hill's *Secrets of Plant Propagation* (Garden Way Publishing, 1985).

For many self-sowing species like ageratum, forget-me-not, and foxglove one has only to catch the seeds before they are naturally dispersed. The most challenging ornamental for the seed-saving flower gardener is double stock, the procedure for which involves a complicated process of selection (and considerable luck).

Unlike with vegetables, there are significant intravarietal differences between some flower varieties. For instance, the cosmos variety 'Sensation Mix' includes four flower colors. When saving seed from year to year from the entire group together, plants with darker flower colors may come to predominate. Commercial seed producers isolate the color strains within the variety for seed growing and then blend the seeds for sale. The home seed grower can partly overcome this problem by saving more seed from the genetically recessive colors (usually the lighter pigments). True zealots may resort to caging seed parents to exclude pollinating insects and to performing hand pollinations. The inheritance pattern of many significant ornamental qualities like doubleness of flowers, flower color, flower shape, and plant stature are extremely complex genetically and not entirely understood. You will have to accept "pot luck" in some cases.

Seed maturation may take several weeks beyond the time the flowers fade. In the meantime the plants may become unsightly and continued flowering will be suppressed in those species where "deadheading" is required. Many gardeners do not harvest seed until the plants have been killed by frost. Freezing temperatures will not kill the seed, but much of your control over seed saving is gone after a frost. Remember to dry the fruits and/or seeds adequately after harvest, even if they appear dry already.

Finally, I will reveal the most important secret of successful flower seed saving: an intimate knowledge and understanding of the plants. Carefully observe them throughout their life cycles. Study the flowers as they expand, dissect an immature ovary to see the ovules and how they are placed, look at the pollen under a microscope, watch the pollinators at work, keep a record of when your favorites flower and the number of days to seed maturity. In other words, get to know as much about the flowers as your time and interest allows. Your diligence will be rewarded in many ways.

AGERATUM (*Ageratum houstonianum,* fam. Asteraceae). Annual. Cross-pollinated by insects.

This old-time favorite can be a prolific self-sower. The seed is tiny (about 200,000 to the ounce!). The flower heads turn brown and dry out as the seed matures. Requires close watch of the seed head or seeds will be lost to shattering.

The many F_1 hybrids will yield variable offspring. 'Blue Mink' is a fine variety from which to save seed.

ALYSSUM, Sweet (*Lobularia maritima,* fam. Brassicaceae). Annual. Cross-pollinated by insects.

This diminutive member of the Mustard Family has a lot to recommend it, being very hardy and blooming only six weeks from seed. In mild climates it may act as a perennial.

The fruit is a small two-celled capsule. The seed matures unevenly over the plant, so you must hand-harvest the capsules when they turn brown (and while damp, to avoid seed loss from shattering.)

AMARANTHUS (*Amaranthus caudatus,* fam. Amaranthaceae). Annual. Monoecious (having separate male and female flowers on the same plant). Wind-pollinated, but generally inbred.

This is an interesting species because of the many horticultural forms, including the varieties 'Love-Lies-Bleeding', 'Green Thumb', 'Pygmy Torch', and 'Viridis'. The male and female flowers are borne adjacent on the flower stalks. Amaranth can be a self-sower, but it requires a long season to mature seed. The fruits are one-seeded, maturing along the flower spikes or "tails."

Red leaves are dominant to green leaves. The young leaves and seeds of this species are edible.

ASTER, China (*Callistephus chinensis,* fam. Asteraceae). Annual. Cross-pollinated by insects, but double-flowered types are mainly self-pollinated.

The China aster is a favorite for cut flowers. Be certain to grow wilt-resistant varieties, since wilt is a seed-borne disease.

Superdouble flowers will not produce seed. Color dominance is purple over red over pink over white. Therefore, purple crossed with red will produce an all-purple F_1. Remember, though, that this F_1 will pass on the red gene 50 percent of the time. Therefore it is possible to cross a purple-flowered plant with a red-flowered plant and obtain 50 percent purple plants and 50 percent red plants. The red-flowered plants obtained will only produce red-flowered plants if pollinated only among themselves.

The seed heads are harvested individually when mature dandelion-like "feathers" appear.

BABY'S-BREATH (*Gypsophila elegans,* fam. Caryophyllaceae). Annual. Cross-pollinated by insects.

The seeds of baby's-breath are ready to harvest when the fruit capsules turn brown. If very mature, it is best to pick the capsules when the dew is on them, to prevent seed loss.

BACHELOR'S-BUTTON (*Centaurea cyanus,* fam. Asteraceae). Annual. Cross-pollinated by insects.

This occasional self-sower sometimes lives over the winter. Flower

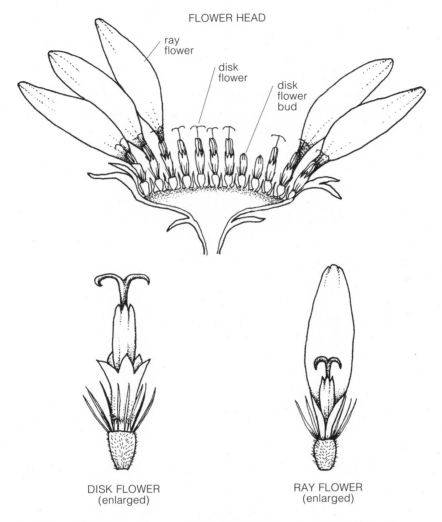

FLOWER HEAD

ray
flower

disk
flower

disk
flower
bud

DISK FLOWER
(enlarged)

RAY FLOWER
(enlarged)

A typical composite flower of the Aster Family, showing both disk and ray flowers.

color dominance is blue over pink over white.

Harvest the seed by cutting when most of the flowering is done; the seed shatters easily, so be careful harvesting it. Birds also enjoy this seed, so beware of losing it to them.

BALSAM, Garden (*Impatiens balsamina,* fam. Balsaminaceae). Annual. Cross-pollinated by insects.

This is a shade-tolerant, moisture-loving relative of the weed touch-me-not or jewelweed. There are many genes which affect flower color and flower form, but in general colors are dominant to white and single flowers are dominant to common double forms.

Harvest the seed-bearing capsules when they are yellow. It is a good idea to put them in an airy covered box, because the seed may be exploded out of the fruit when dry.

BEAN, Scarlet Runner (*Phaseolus coccineus,* fam. Fabaceae). Annual. Self-pollinated.

This ornamental bean is grown like regular pole beans. It is a perennial in the Tropics, where it was probably the original edible bean of the Aztecs. Many modern stringless varieties are available for table use. Pods can reach one foot long, and seeds to one inch wide. The selection var. *albus* has white flowers. The flowers are self-pollinated, so red and white varieties can be maintained together. See the Bean entry on page 98 for further seed-growing information.

BELLS-OF-IRELAND (*Moluccella laevis,* fam. Labiatae). Annual. Cross-pollinated by insects.

The showy part of this plant is the persistent *calyx* (the external part of the flower, consisting of the sepals). The fragrant flowers are tiny. The seeds are in the collection of four nutlets nestled within the base of the calyx. Seeds are ready for harvest when the nutlets are dry. Seeds may self-sow.

Germination of this species may be difficult. Best results have been obtained by pre-chilling soaked seeds at 50°F. (10°C.) for five days, then germinating them at temperatures of 50°F. (10°C.) at night, 85°F. (30°C.) during the day. It may take up to three weeks for germination to occur.

BORAGE (*Borago officinalis,* fam. Boraginaceae). Annual. Cross-pollinated by insects.

Borage is a marvelous bee plant. The plant is rather coarse, but has lovely blue flowers (occasionally purple or white). The flower can be candied as a confection. The leaves, which have a cucumbery flavor, can be used in soups, salads, etc. *Borago* is derived from the Latin *burra,* 'rough' or 'hairy', which describes the foliage. Seed savers should look for a hairless strain, which would be welcomed by all borage eaters.

The species sometimes self-sows. Harvest the seed when the one-seeded nutlets are dry (occasionally two-seeded nutlets occur).

CABBAGE, Flowering (*Brassica oleracea,* Acephala Group, fam. Brassicaceae). Biennial. Cross-pollinated by insects.

This ornamental is grown for seed like the regular vegetable cabbage, except that it does not form a tight head. See Cabbage, page 75.

CALENDULA (*Calendula officinalis,* fam. Asteraceae). Annual. Cross-pollinated by insects.

The calendula or pot marigold has been a garden favorite for centuries. In cool regions the plants have a very long flowering season if dead heads are promptly removed.

The full double-flowered varieties may be sterile, because of a lack of stamens early in the season, but later the flowers may become fertile semi-doubles.

Hybrids like 'Mandarin F_1' and 'Apricot Sherbet F_1' will not come true from saved seed, but may segregate out some interesting individuals. The "seed" of the calendula is actually the fruit.

Cut the flower heads before the seeds shatter. The seeds can be slightly immature when harvested.

CANDYTUFT, Globe (*Iberis umbellata,* fam. Brassicaceae). Annual. Cross-pollinated by insects.

This hardy annual will sometimes overwinter when sowed late. It blooms six weeks from sowing until hard frost. Flower colors are white to purple.

Sometimes the outer flowers in a cluster are sterile. Harvest the small, roundish pods when they turn a yellowish brown. Each pod compartment contains one seed. The seeds do not shatter. Alternate wetting and drying of the pod will make seed extraction easier.

CANTERBURY-BELLS (*Campanula medium,* fam. Campanulaceae). Biennial. Cross-pollinated by insects.

There are various forms of this plant other than the normal bell-flower. An annual variety is available. Flower color ranges from violet to white, with darker colors dominant over lighter ones. The double forms do not come totally true from seed.

The cup-and-saucer variety has a flared series of outer "petals," with the inner petals forming the regular bell, and the "hose-in-hose" type that has a bell within a bell; both are partially dominant over the normal bellflower type.

This species may be difficult to overwinter in severe climates. Rabbits are attracted to it as a gustatory treat.

The tiny seeds (120,000 per ounce) are dispersed from slits at the base of the fruit capsule when mature. The seeds may take two to three weeks or more to germinate.

CELOSIA (*Celosia cristata,* fam. Amaranthaceae). Annual. Monoecious (having separate male and female flowers on the same plant). Wind-pollinated.

These ornamentals are considered weeds in the Tropics. The species includes the cockscomb type and the feathered (*plumosa*) type, both available in some fiery reds and brilliant golds.

Harvest the seeds when they have dried within the flower heads. Sift them through screening, to separate chaff.

CHRYSANTHEMUM (*Chrysanthemum* spp., fam. Asteraceae). Annual. Cross-pollinated by insects.

There are several species of these relatives of the florist's chrysanthemum including the crown daisy *(C. coronarium)* and the most popular corn marigold *(C. segetum)*. There are several named varieties of each available. The species *C. carinatum* has a variety, 'Court Jesters Mixed', with flowers in many different brilliant colors.

Cut the flower heads when they are dry, and be careful not to let the seed shatter.

CLARKIA (*Clarkia unguiculata,* fam. Onagraceae). Annual. Self-pollinated.

This native of the western United States was named for Captain William Clark of Lewis and Clark fame. The very showy flowers come in many shades ranging from purple to white. The darker colors seem to dominate in intercrosses, as do double flowers. Commercial growers isolate different varieties by 200 feet.

The seeds are ready to harvest as soon as the lower capsules begin to open. Seeds may be easily shaken out of the fruits.

GODETIA *(Clarkia amoena)* can be treated similarly.

COSMOS (*Cosmos bipinnatus,* fam. Asteraceae). Annual. Cross-pollinated by insects.

This is deservedly a favorite for the back of annual gardens and for cut flowers. When selecting seed parents, be aware that the darker colors dominate the lighter colors in a cross.

You may notice some of the "petals" have a splash of color at the base, lacking in other flowers. The base color gene is also dominant. There are double-flowered forms and a variety with tubular ray flowers (outside "petals") called 'Sea Shells'. The variety 'Candy Stripe' has red-and-white-striped flowers.

The so-called Klondike cosmos belongs to the species *Cosmos sulphureus* and will not cross with *C. bipinnatus.*

To harvest seed, pick the entire head as it ripens. Dry the head and roll the seeds out.

COREOPSIS, Golden (*Coreopsis tinctoria,* fam. Asteraceae). Annual. Cross-pollinated by insects.

Also known as calliopsis, this is the most popular of the annual coreopsis species. Yellow flower color is dominant to brown. The flower heads ripen unevenly, so one must watch carefully as the seed matures and harvest individual heads as the seed dries.

DAISY, English (*Bellis perennis,* fam. Asteraceae). Biennial. Cross-pollinated by insects.

This is the common garden daisy of Shakespeare's time and before. It is a weedy perennial in England, where it often self-sows.

The special varieties like those with quilled (tubular) ray flowers (the outside "petals") and double flowers do not come true from seed.

The seeds are tiny, at 135,000 per ounce. Harvest the seed heads when they are dry, before the seed shatters.

DAISY, Gloriosa (*Rudbeckia hirta,* fam. Asteraceae). Annual or biennial. Cross-pollinated by insects.

The garden variety of this species is the tetraploid form of the black-eyed Susan. It often self-seeds, so harvest the flower heads before the seed is dispersed. It may take up to three weeks for seed to germinate. It is possible to obtain a (probably) sterile triploid form if the plant crosses with wild black-eyed Susan.

DAISY, Swan River (*Brachycome iberidifolia,* fam. Asteraceae). Annual. Cross-pollinated by insects.

This Australian native prefers a cool climate. The flower colors vary from purple to white, with the darker colors dominant. Harvest the individual flower heads as they mature and before the seed falls.

FLAX, Flowering (*Linum grandiflorum,* fam. Linaceae). Annual. Cross-pollinated by insects.

This is a red- or pink-flowering species related to the important fiber plant which supplies the raw materials for linen and linseed oil.

The fruit is a capsule, usually containing 10 seeds. Harvest the fruits when they are dry, but before they split open.

FORGET-ME-NOT (*Myosotis sylvatica,* fam. Boraginaceae). Annual or biennial. Cross-pollinated by insects.

This little, usually blue-flowered plant is also available in red, pink and white forms, with the darker colors dominant. It can become a weedy pest due to self-sowing. I have had spots where it apparently died out, and then years later it reappeared. Sow in the summer for flowers next spring. Sown early in the year, it may produce flowers that year.

The fruit is a collection of four nutlets which are harvested before they drop.

Some varieties of *M. sylvatica* are incorrectly listed in seed catalogs as belonging to the species *M. alpestris*.

FOUR-O'CLOCK (*Mirabilis jalapa,* fam. Nyctaginaceae). Annual; may persist as a perennial. Cross-pollinated by insects.

This plant puts on its show as a daily late matinee. It may persist as a perennial in southern climates. The tuberous roots, similar to those of dahlia, can be lifted and stored over the winter in the North.

Taller forms are dominant to dwarf forms. Flower color is inherited in a complex manner.

The leathery fruits contain one seed, harvested as they dry. The plant may self-sow.

Hummingbirds are particularly attracted to four-o'clocks.

FOXGLOVE (*Digitalis purpurea,* fam. Scrophulariaceae). Biennial. Cross-pollinated by insects.

Foxglove is one of the most commonly cultivated biennials since it is easy to grow and quite showy. There are many forms: one with a terminal flower like a morning-glory, one with leopard-like spots on the flowers, a double-flowered type, one that blooms the first year, and various cultivars with flower colors ranging from purple to white.

All parts of the plant are poisonous, it being the source of the common heart medication, digitalis.

The flower spikes are quite long, so lower fruit capsules may be dropping their many tiny seeds while the flowers are still open above. Watch the plants for opening of the lower fruits and begin to harvest seed at that time. Foxglove will self-sow in masses that have to be thinned out.

GAILLARDIA (*Gaillardia pulchella,* fam. Asteraceae). Annual. Cross-pollinated by insects.

Also known as the annual blanket flower, gaillardia has a bright and showy daisy-like flower, ranging in color from yellow to purplish orange (and reportedly a white form).

It may self-sow; otherwise, harvest the heads as they mature and roll the seed out. Germination may take several weeks.

HOLLYHOCK (*Alcea rosea,* fam. Malvaceae). Annual, biennial, perennial. Cross-pollinated by insects.

If you picture in your mind's eye an English or early American cottage garden, hollyhocks should be a main feature. The genus was formerly called *Althaea,* but has now changed to *Alcea.*

The special annual strains must be started very early. The regular hollyhock is a perennial, but it is best treated as a biennial.

The double-flowered varieties are incompletely dominant over the singles, and crosses will yield in the F_1 all semi-doubles. The F_2 would segregate out doubles, semi-doubles, and singles in the ratio of 1:2:1.

Fruits are ready to harvest two to three weeks after flowering. The fruit consists of the seeds collected in a circle, which will disintegrate into the individual seeds and chaff if handled when dry. Seeds take two to three weeks to germinate.

HONESTY (*Lunaria annua,* fam. Brassicaceae). Annual or biennial. Cross-pollinated by insects.

Hollyhock *(Alcea rosea).*

FRUIT

FLOWERING STEM

SEED

This easily grown species is popular because of the remnant of the dried flower that is used in arrangements. However, the biennial forms may need winter protection.

The white-margined leaf type 'Albomarginata' is recessive to the normal.

The few seeds per flower are borne on each side of the papery partition which divides the pod. The seeds are mature when the pods are dry. Collect before the outer pod cases fall away. Honesty may self-sow.

KALE, Flowering (*Brassica oleracea*, Acephala Group, fam. Brassicaceae). Biennial. Cross-pollinated by insects.

This ornamental is grown for seed in the same manner as the vegetable kale. Refer to the Kale entry on p. 85.

LARKSPUR, Annual (*Consolida orientalis*, fam. Ranunculaceae). Annual. Cross-pollinated by insects.

This species was formerly known as *Delphinium ajacis*. The juice and seeds are poisonous.

Darker flower colors are dominant. Harvest the seeds as soon as the lower capsules begin to open. The seed is easily shaken out of the end of the fruit. It may readily self-sow.

Larkspur germinates in about three weeks in the dark (light is reported to inhibit germination).

LOBELIA, Annual (*Lobelia erinus*, fam. Lobeliaceae). Annual. Cross-pollinated by insects.

This is a popular edging plant with many horticultural forms, including compact shape and double flowers (full doubles are sterile).

Usually blue-flowered, it is available in other colors, too. 'Cambridge Blue' is the most popular variety. The plant is poisonous if eaten.

The fruit is a two-part capsule containing many tiny seeds (about 700,000 per ounce). Harvest when the capsules are dry and thresh by shaking in a paper bag.

Lobelia takes up to three weeks to germinate.

LOVE-IN-A-MIST (*Nigella damascena,* fam. Ranunculaceae). Annual. Cross-pollinated by insects.

This is an old-fashioned favorite grown for both its attractive flowers and its dried fruits, which are used in arrangements. The seed was used like pepper long ago.

Flower colors range from purple to white, with darker colors dominant in a complex genetic pattern. Single flowers and tall stature are both dominant to their alternatives.

The fruit is an inflated capsule containing many seeds dispersed through an opening at the top. Harvest as the fruits dry and shake out the seeds.

LUPINE, Dwarf (*Lupinus nanus,* fam. Fabaceae). Annual. Self-pollinated.

The little pealike pods are harvested as they turn brown. Each pod contains five to six flat, hard, kidney-shaped, shatter-prone seeds. The seeds should be nicked carefully through the seed coat with a file to hasten germination. Other lupine species are treated similarly.

MALLOW, Rose (*Lavatera trimestris,* fam. Malvaceae). Annual. Cross-pollinated by insects.

This is a close relative of the hollyhock and looks it. Despite the common name, there is a white-flowered form.

The seeds occur within a cluster of podlike fruitlets, one seed per fruit. Harvest the fruit when it is dry, and do not extract the seed from the fruit, just separate the fruitlets.

Seeds may take up to three weeks to germinate.

MARIGOLD (*Tagetes* species, fam. Asteraceae). Annual. Cross-pollinated by insects.

The marigold is one of the most popular annual plants and hence receives much attention from plant breeders and seed growers. Burpee's search for the white marigold will go down in the annals of commercial horticulture as a brilliant advertising campaign.

The French marigold *(Tagetes patula)* is not really French but Mexican and is tetraploid. The African or American marigold *(Tagetes erecta)* is also of Mexican origin and is a diploid. Commercial crosses between the big American and the little French marigold produce a sterile triploid hybrid with the huge flower of the former and the dwarfness of the latter, but with poor seed germination.

There are many F_1 hybrids available which will not come true from seed.

Doubleness of the flowers is a dominant trait. The extreme double may produce little pollen and so must be pollinated by another variety. As the flower season progresses, double-flowering plants may begin to produce semi-double and single flowers, which will be fertile within the variety.

Harvest the seeds when the individual heads dry. Seed is easily rubbed from the head.

MORNING-GLORY (*Ipomoea purpurea*, fam. Convolvulaceae). Annual. Cross-pollinated by insects.

This viny near-weed will not produce its beautiful flowers if the soil is too moist or too fertile. The double-flowered forms are dominant over singles. Inheritance of flower color is complex. I would stick with one color — like the aptly named 'Heavenly Blue'.

The fruit is a globe-shaped capsule usually containing about six large seeds with very hard coats, which must be nicked with a file or soaked in warm water overnight to hasten germination. Morning-glory may self-sow. Harvest the fruits when they are dry and break open the capsule to obtain the seeds.

MOSS ROSE (*Portulaca grandiflora,* fam. Portulacaceae). Annual. Cross-pollinated by insects.

This is a close relative of the common weed purslane or pusley, but will not be troublesome like it. Portulaca will thrive even with poor soil and in drought conditions.

Inheritance of flower color is complex, but doubleness of flow-ers is inherited as a simple dominant.

The fruit is a capsule with many tiny seeds (about 280,000 seeds per ounce). The seed is dispersed through a hinged lid atop the capsule. Harvest the seeds when the capsule is dry.

NASTURTIUM (*Tropaeolum majus,* fam. Tropaeolaceae). Annual. Cross-pollinated by insects.

The nasturtium has a long history of breeding manipulation, so to-day there are many colors; long-trailing and compact vines; single, double, and superdouble flowers; and green or variegated foliage.

Do not plant nasturtiums in too fertile a soil, or flowering will be sparse. Be watchful for heterosporium leaf spot, a seed-borne disease.

The fruit is three-celled, with each cell containing one seed. Harvest when the fruit is dry and separate the three cells. Seed is not extracted from the individual cell. Nasturtium sometimes self-sows.

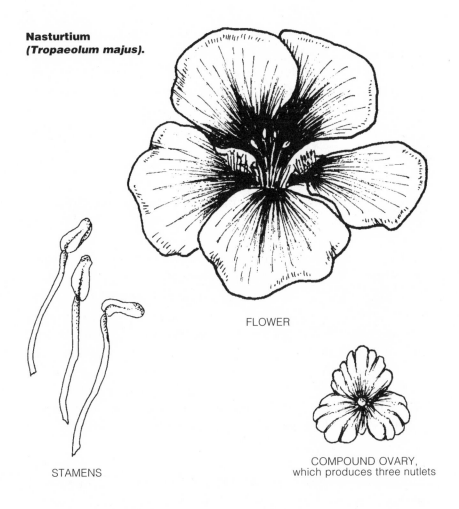

**Nasturtium
(*Tropaeolum majus*).**

FLOWER

STAMENS

COMPOUND OVARY,
which produces three nutlets

PANSY (*Viola* x *wittrockiana,* fam. Violaceae). Annual, biennial, or undependable perennial. Cross-pollinated by insects.

The pansy used to be known as *Viola tricolor hortensis,* but those in the know decided that it is actually a hybrid between *V. lutea* and *V. tricolor,* hence the new epithet.

Seed saved from some varieties, particularly the F_1 hybrids, reverts to inferior forms. Flower color is inherited in a complex manner. Be watchful for pansy anthracnose, because it can be perpetuated via the seed.

Though the species is cross-pollinated by insects, I have gathered mature seed from plants in the greenhouse where no pollinators were active. Handpick the fruit capsules as they mature. Put the closed capsules in a box covered with cloth. As they dry, the seeds will be ejected.

PETUNIA (*Petunia* x *hybrida*, fam. Solanaceae). Annual. Cross-pollinated by insects.

The petunia is one of those species on which the hybridizers have spent much effort — with wonderful success. This species, actually a perennial, includes the types advertised as *P. grandiflora, P. floribunda,* and *P. multiflora.* They are easily intercrossed and produce various types of offspring. The breeders have yet to produce a strain that will really stand up to rainstorms.

Double-flowered varieties are usually female sterile, but they do produce viable pollen, which can be transferred to single flowers. Seedling doubles are usually more vigorous, with thicker stems than singles.

Be watchful for the tobacco ringspot virus, which is a seed-borne disease that affects petunias.

In general, later flowers produce larger, healthier fruits. Harvest the capsules when they are dry, but before they split open. Each capsule contains 100 to 300 seeds. Petunia commonly self-sows and quickly reverts to a wild form.

PHLOX, Annual (*Phlox drummondii,* fam. Polemoniaceae). Annual. Cross-pollinated by insects.

A high percentage of self-pollination occurs in phlox. Flower color is inherited in a complex manner. The so-called salver-shaped flower is dominant to the funnel-shaped flower.

The fruit is a three-celled capsule, with each cell usually maturing only one seed. Harvest when the capsules begin to turn brown.

PINK (*Dianthus chinensis,* fam. Caryophyllaceae). Annual, biennial, perennial. Cross-pollinated by insects.

The China or India pink is now available in various F_1 hybrid varieties which will revert to an unimproved type.

A wet growing season may ruin the seed crop. The seed usually matures early in September. The fruit is a capsule, which becomes brown and very hard as it matures. Harvest the capsules and continue to dry for another two weeks. The capsules will split open to free the seeds.

POPPY, California (*Eschscholzia californica,* fam. Papaveraceae). Annual. Cross-pollinated by insects.

This poppy is the California state flower, occurring in shades of white, orange, red, and bicolors. The colorless sap is said to be mildly narcotic and to have been used by Indians in California as a treatment for toothaches.

Heterosporium leaf spot or capsule spot is a seed-borne disease to watch out for.

The fruit is a many-seeded, cone-shaped pod three to four inches long. Harvest the fruit when the capsules turn a light brown, before the seed shatters. California poppy may self-sow.

POPPY, Opium (*Papaver somniferum,* fam. Papaveraceae). Annual. Cross-pollinated by insects.

This is the controversial poppy of the heroin trade. Crude opium is

**California Poppy
(*Eschscholzia calfornica*).**

the hardened milky sap exuded from slits made in the unripe fruits.

Flower color dominance is purple over red over white. Individuals in the F_2 may vary a great deal in color shading.

Single flowers are dominant over double flowers.

POPPY, Shirley (*Papaver rhoeas,* fam. Papaveraceae). Annual. Pollinated by insects.

This is the famous poppy of Flanders' fields. It is a prolific self-seeder. Different varieties of this species are available in many colors ranging from red to purple to white. Inheritance of flower color is complex.

Harvest the seed when the fruit capsules begin to open, but before the seed is dispersed.

ROCKET, Sweet or Dame's (*Hesperis matronalis,* fam. Brassicaceae). Biennial. Cross-pollinated by insects.

This is an undependable perennial best treated as a biennial. Flower color comes in shades of purple and plain white. The flowers are very fragrant, especially at night. Double flower varieties also exist.

Seedpods are two to four inches long and contain a row of seeds. Harvest when the pods are dry.

SALPIGLOSSIS (*Salpiglossis sinuata,* fam. Solanaceae). Annual. Cross-pollinated by insects.

One can see the resemblance of these flowers to petunias, to which they are related. The large, velvety, trumpet-shaped flowers come in a variety of colors. This species is difficult to grow in hot climates.

The fruit is a capsule containing many minute seeds. Harvest when the capsules are dry, before the seed shatters.

Seed will germinate in two weeks.

SALVIA (*Salvia splendens,* fam. Lamiaceae). Annual. Cross-pollinated by insects.

Salvia is actually a tender perennial subshrub, but it is grown as an annual. Flower colors include red, purple, and white. One seed is contained within each of several nutlets that form at the base of the flower. Harvest when the nutlets are dry, before the fruit drops. Salvia may self-sow.

It takes up to two weeks for seed to germinate.

SCABIOUS, Sweet (*Scabiosa atropurpurea,* fam. Dipsacaceae). Annual. Cross-pollinated by insects.

Also known as the pincushion flower, this hardy plant is available in flower colors shading from purple through pink to white. There are double-flowered types, and the variety 'Grandiflora' has larger flower heads.

The flowers are attractive to hummingbirds.

The "seeds" cohere in the head and can be harvested when the head dries. Don't wait too long, however, as the "seeds" are wind-dispersed.

Seeds take up to two weeks to germinate.

SNAPDRAGON (*Antirrhinum majus,* fam. Scrophulariaceae). Annual. Self-pollinated.

The snapdragon is actually a perennial, treated as an annual. It can be propagated by cuttings. It is mainly self-pollinated, but it is amusing to watch bumblebees force their way through the tight lips of the flower to access the nectar.

In general, the darker colors are the most dominant genetically. Yellow, not white, is said to be the most recessive.

Plant breeders have had great success with this species, so

there is much diversity. Varieties are available as F_1 and F_2 hybrids, as well as tetraploids, only the last of which will come true from saved seed.

The fruit is a capsule containing many seeds. Cut the flower stalk when two-thirds of the capsules are ripe for a large seed harvest. Otherwise, harvest the individual fruits and shake out the seeds. Snapdragon sometimes self-sows. The seeds are tiny, at 180,000 per ounce. Germination may take up to three weeks.

SNOW-ON-THE-MOUNTAIN (*Euphorbia marginata,* fam. Euphorbiaceae). Annual. Monoecious (having separate male and female flowers on the same plant). Cross-pollinated by insects.

This close relative of poinsettia is a morphologically peculiar plant. The showy parts of the plant are leaflike white bracts. The true flowers, male and female, are inconspicuous.

The fruit is a small capsule containing usually three seeds. Harvest the fruits and extract the seeds when mature. Fruits may open explosively. This plant can self-sow and become weedy.

Many people suffer an allergic reaction following skin contact with the milky sap.

SPIDER FLOWER (*Cleome hasslerana,* fam. Capparaceae). Annual. Cross-pollinated by insects.

Spider flower and cosmos together make a terrific backdrop for the annual border, with a pastel color splash that waves in the breeze. Spider flowers are available in shades of white, pink, and light purple.

The fruits are long slender "pods" that stick out of the stem like whiskers. Harvest the pods individually and extract the seeds before they are dispersed. Spider flower can be a self-sower. The seeds may take up to two weeks to germinate.

STOCK (*Matthiola incana,* fam. Brassicaceae). Annual or biennial. Mainly self-pollinated.

The stock is a challenge to the gardener and seed saver. The annual forms include ten-weeks stocks and seven-weeks stocks, the latter of which is *trisomic,* having one or a few triploid chromosomes in its otherwise diploid set. They all do best with a continuously cool season. Bacterial blight is a seed-borne disease in stock.

The problem for the seed saver is in obtaining the double-flowering types, which set no seed. One must save seed from the so-called "single-flowered, double-throwing" stocks, which give about 50 percent doubles. In the seedling stage, the dark green individuals will be single-flowered and the lighter green ones will produce double flowers.

Trial and error and copious record keeping and luck will help you select a double-throwing strain of single stocks from your original seed source of mixed doubles and singles. Some bedding plant growers have single-flowered stocks available that may be double-throwing.

The fruit is a pod containing 30 to 60 seeds. Harvest when mature.

SUNFLOWER (*Helianthus annuus,* fam. Asteraceae). Annual. Cross-pollinated by insects.

This plant, some forms of which can grow to astounding heights in the space of one year, is the source of the common bird seed.

The "seed," which is technically the fruit, is massed in the flat heads that can be a foot or more across. Harvest the seed when it is dry, before it drops. The birds may beat you to it. Weevils occasionally infest the seed.

The sunflower can be a prolific self-sower.

SWEET PEA (*Lathyrus odoratus,* fam. Fabaceae). Annual. Self-pollinated.

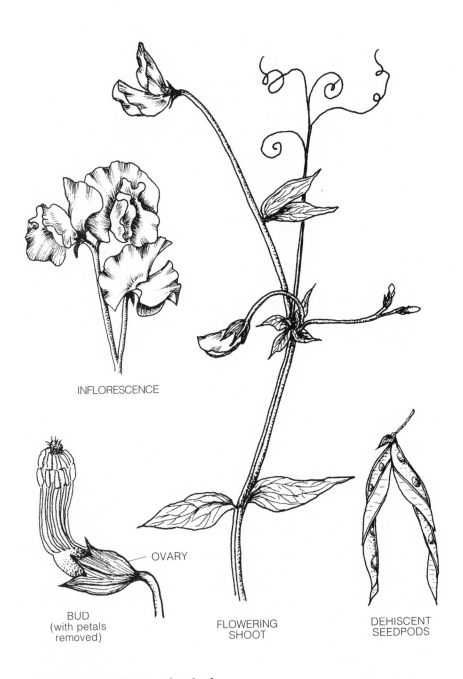

INFLORESCENCE

OVARY

BUD
(with petals
removed)

FLOWERING
SHOOT

DEHISCENT
SEEDPODS

Sweet Pea *(Lathyrus odoratus).*

These sweet-scented climbers used to be garden favorites. They are too little grown today.

There are various flower colors, plant heights, and flower forms, all of which have complex inheritance patterns. Anthracnose and bacterial streak are both seed-borne diseases to watch for.

If you would like to try your hand at plant breeding, sweet peas are fun to work with. The technique is simple: first, choose a nearly mature flower that has not shed its pollen. Carefully remove all the anthers with a pair of forceps, without injuring the other floral organs. The stigma will not be receptive, but pollen from the male parent can be gently placed on it at this time. The final step is to tag the flower with the parentage and the date indicated in pencil. For example: 6/15, White x Red. When the dry pods are harvested the record keeping must continue, and when the seeds are planted, too. The F_1 flower color from your cross White x Red will come to light.

Seeds germinate in about two weeks, if soaked overnight before planting.

SWEET WILLIAM (*Dianthus barbatus,* fam. Caryophyllaceae). Biennial. Cross-pollinated by insects.

This sprightly member of the Pink Family is actually a short-lived perennial. The annual form 'Wee Willie' double comes true from seed when pollinated by a double.

The fruit is a small capsule containing many seeds. Harvest before the seed shatters.

TOBACCO, Flowering (*Nicotiana alata,* fam. Solanaceae). Annual. Cross-pollinated by insects.

This long-blooming, floriferous member of the Nightshade Family is actually a perennial. The variety 'Grandiflora', in fact, is propagated by root cuttings.

Flower color is complex genetically, but in general darker colors are dominant.

The fruit is a small capsule containing many minute seeds (about 350,000 per ounce). It often self-sows, so one must pick the fruits before the seed shatters. The seed germinates in about 15 days.

VERBENA (*Verbena* x *hybrida,* fam. Verbenaceae). Annual. Cross-pollinated by insects.

Verbena, one of the best all-season bloomers, is actually a perennial. The species is quite variable, and there are a number of varieties which will intercross and produce something different.

The fruit consists of a small number of one-seeded nutlets. The seed germinates in about three weeks.

WALLFLOWER (*Cheiranthus cheiri,* fam. Brassicaceae). Annual or biennial. Limited cross-pollination by insects.

Pronounced Ky RAN' thus, this plant is a perennial in England.

Darker color shades are dominant. Double-flowered types set little or no seed. Special flower colors and forms are propagated by cuttings or division.

The fruit is a pod 2 to 2½ inches long. Seeds are mature when the pod yellows.

The *Erysimum* species wallflowers are similar to *Cheiranthus.*

ZINNIA (*Zinnia elegans,* fam. Asteraceae). Annual. Cross-pollinated by insects.

This is my favorite flower for bright, long-lasting summer bouquets. The plant breeders have worked hard to make many varieties of this very popular bloomer available. Today there are many F_1 hybrids to choose from, but they are not recommended for the seed saver.

Be watchful for zinnia blight, which is seed-borne. It would be good to select a strain resistant to the unsightly alternaria leaf spot.

The seed is mature when the flower has dried up. The seed sticks tightly to the central core, and requires some effort to remove it.

Mail-Order
Seed Sources

The following is a select list of companies — some large, some small — that should be of interest to seed savers, either because of the wide selection they offer or because they carry seeds of particular interest: old-time or seldom-seen varieties, foreign seed strains, or seeds that are well-adapted to a particular growing region or climate of North America. While most of the companies listed specialize in vegetable seeds, many of the larger mail-order sources also offer flower seeds and plants in their catalogs.

This list is by no means complete. Serious seed savers will want to buy a copy of the standard reference from which this list is adapted — the *Garden Seed Inventory, 2nd Edition,* published by

Seed Savers Exchange, RR 3, Box 239, Decorah, Iowa 52101. This 418-page reference lists and describes more than 5,000 vegetable seed varieties found in some 240 catalogs. The *Garden Seed Inventory* is available from Seed Savers Exchange for $17.50 softcover or $25.00 hardcover, postage paid.

One final note. Garden seed companies are like most other kinds of businesses: over the course of years, some may change ownership, discontinue product lines, and even go out of business. The following selection of seed suppliers is presented as the most current information available as of this printing. Any corrections submitted by readers will be added to the updates to be used for future printings of *Savings Seeds*.

ABUNDANT LIFE SEED FOUNDATION
P.O. Box 772
Port Townsend, WA 98368
$5.00 for seed catalog, book list, and periodic newsletters.
Untreated seeds for the Northwest Pacific rim.

ALBERTA NURSERIES & SEEDS LTD.
Box 20, Bowden, Alberta
T0M 0K0, Canada
(800) 733-3566
Free catalog. Seeds for short-season areas.

STERLING AND LOTHROP
191 U.S. Rte. 1
Falmouth, ME 04105
$1.00 for catalog, refundable with order. Vegetable seeds adapted to northern New England. Company founded in 1911.

W. ATLEE BURPEE CO.
300 Park Ave.
Warminster, PA 18974
(800) 888-1447
Free catalog. The largest mail-order seed source in the United States, with a huge selection.

BURRELL SEED GROWERS CO.
Box 150
Rocky Ford, CO 81067
$1.00 for catalog, refundable with order. Family-owned business founded in 1900. Fine selection of cantaloupes and watermelons.

COMSTOCK, FERRE & CO.
263 Main St.
Wethersfield, CT 06109
(800) 733-3773
Free catalog. Established in 1820. 320 vegetable varieties, including many older varieties.

THE COOK'S GARDEN
P.O. Box 535
Londonderry, VT 05148
(800) 457-9705
*Catalog free. Specializing in
greens, with 50 varieties of lettuce,
many seldom-seen. Also offers
other culinary vegetables.*

WILLIAM DAM SEEDS LTD.
Box 8400, Dundas, Ontario
L9H 6M1, Canada
*$2.00 for catalog, refundable with
order. Vegetable, flower, and herb
seeds, featuring many European
varieties.*

DE GIORGI SEED
6011 N St.
Omaha, NE 68117-1634
(800) 858-2580
*$2.00 for catalog. Many unique
and old-time varieties.*

FARMER SEED & NURSERY CO.
1706 Morrissey Dr.
Bloomington, IL 61704
*Free catalog. Specializes in cold-
hardy northern varieties.*

GARDEN CITY SEEDS
778 Hwy 93 North
Hamilton, MT 59840
(406) 961-4837
*Free catalog. Nonprofit company
featuring untreated, organically
grown seeds adapted to the North.*

GURNEY'S SEED & NURSERY CO.
110 Capital St.
Yankton, SD 57079
(605) 665-1671
*Free catalog. Huge selection of
hardy vegetables, flowers, and
nursery stock.*

HARRIS SEEDS
P.O. Box 22960
Rochester, NY 14692-2960
(800) 514-4441
*Free catalog. Exclusive flower and
vegetable seed introductions.*

ED HUME SEEDS
P.O. Box 1450
Kent, WA 98035
(253) 859-1110
*$1.00 for catalog. Seeds for the
Pacific Northwest and short-season
areas. Special collections for Alaska
and fall and winter planting.*

JOHNNY'S SELECTED SEEDS
310 Foss Hill Road
Albion, ME 04910-9731
(207) 437-4301
*Free catalog. Seeds for northern
climates. Many new introductions.*

JUNG SEEDS AND NURSERY
335 South High St.
Randolph, WI 53957
(800) 247-5864
*Established 1907. Vegetable and
flower seeds.*

LANDRETH SEED CO.
180-188 West Ostend St.
Baltimore, MD 21230
(800) 654-2407
*Free catalog. The oldest seed house
in the U.S., founded in 1784.*

MELLINGER'S INC.
2310 W. South Range Rd.
North Lima, OH 44452-9731
(800) 321-7444
*Free catalog. Vegetable, tree, herb,
unusual, and imported seeds.*

NORTHPLAN/MOUNTAIN SEED
P.O. Box 9107
Moscow, ID 83843-1607
$1.00 for catalog, refundable with first order. Native seed list. Cold-hardy seeds adapted to short seasons or higher elevations.

PARK SEED CO.
Cokesbury Road
Greenwood, SC 29647
(800) 845-3369
Free catalog. Flower seed specialists since 1868. Also carries a full line of vegetables.

PINETREE GARDEN SEEDS
Box 300
New Gloucester, ME 04260
(270) 926-3400
Free catalog. Specializing in varieties for limited space, with some unique offerings.

PLANTS OF THE SOUTHWEST
Agua Fria
Route 6, Box 11A
Santa Fe, NM 87501
$3.50 for catalog. Featuring little-known Native American plants and drought-tolerant vegetables for the Southwest.

REDWOOD CITY SEED CO.
P.O. Box 361
Redwood City, CA 94064
$1.00 for catalog. Rare and unique varieties.

RICHTERS
357 Highway 47
Goodwood, Ontario
L0C 1A0, Canada
Free catalog. Family-owned company featuring 400 types of herbs, unusual gourmet vegetables.

SEEDS BLÜM
Idaho City Stage
Boise, ID 83706
(208) 342-0858
$3.00 for catalog ($4.50 for 1st class mail). Over 700 heirloom varieties, including unusual potatoes.

R.H. SHUMWAY SEEDSMAN
P.O. Box 1
Graniteville, SC 29829
(803) 663-9771
$1.00 for catalog, refundable with order. Traditional open-pollinated seed varieties.

**SOUTHERN EXPOSURE
SEED EXCHANGE**
P.O. Box 170
Earlysville, VA 22936
$2.00 for catalog. Many heirloom and open-pollinated varieties, with emphasis on seeds suited to the mid-Atlantic growing region.

SOUTHERN GARDEN CO.
P.O. Box 200 D-6
10800 Alpharetta Hwy.
Roswell, GA 30076
Free catalog. Offers seeds that are well adapted to the Southeast.

STOKES SEEDS INC.
Box 548
Buffalo, NY 14240
(716) 695-6980
Free catalog. Established 1881;
features huge selection of seeds for
home gardeners.

TERRITORIAL SEED CO.
P.O. Box 157
Cottage Grove, OR 97424
(541) 942-9547
Free catalog. Specializes in
varieties suited for Pacific
Maritime climate.

THOMPSON & MORGAN
P.O. Box 1308
Jackson, NJ 08527
(800) 274-7333
Free catalog. U.S. branch of well-
known English seedhouse.
Offering 4,000 different varieties
of vegetable and flower seeds.

TILLINGHAST SEED CO.
P.O. Box 738
La Conner, WA 98257
(206) 466-3552
Call for order information. Seeds
for western Washington and
British Columbia. The oldest
seedhouse in the Northwest,
established in 1885.

TOMATO GROWERS
SUPPLY COMPANY
P.O. Box 2237
Fort Myers, FL 33902
(914) 768-1119
Free catalog. Family-owned
company serving the backyard
tomato grower.

VESEY'S SEEDS LTD.
P.O. Box 9000
Charolettetown
Prince Edward Island
Canada COA IPO
(800) 363-7333
Free catalog. Specializing in
vegetable and flower seeds for
short-season areas.

WILLHITE SEED CO.
P.O. Box 23
Poolville, TX 76487
(800) 457-9703
Free catalog. Large selection of
watermelons and cantaloupes,
including introduced varieties.

Further Reading

Readers who desire to read more about seeds should consult the following books:

Hartmann, Hudson, and Dale E. Kester. *Plant Propagation*. Englewood Cliffs, New Jersey: Prentice-Hall Inc., 1975.

Hawthorn, L.R., and L.H. Pollard. *Vegetable and Flower Seed Production*. New York and Toronto: Plakiston, 1954.

Hill, Lewis. *Secrets of Plant Propagation*. Pownal, Vermont: Garden Way Publishing, 1985.

Knott, James Edward. *Handbook for Vegetable Growers*. New York: John Wiley & Sons, 1962.

Lawrence, W.J.C. *Practical Plant Breeding*. London: Allen and Unwin, Ltd., 1965.

Rickett, Harold William. *Botany for Gardeners*. New York: Macmillan Co., 1957.

Slate, George L., ed. *Handbook on Breeding Ornamental Plants*. New York: Brooklyn Botanic Garden, 1959. (Special issue of *Plants and Gardens*, v. 15, no. 2).

Weatherwax, Paul. *Indian Corn in Old America*. New York: Macmillan Co., 1954.

Whitsin, John, et al., eds. *Luther Burbank, His Methods and Discoveries and Their Practical Application*. New York: Luther Burbank Press, 1914.

U.S. Department of Agriculture. *Seeds, Yearbook of Agriculture 1961*. Washington, D.C.: USDA, 1961.

Glossary for Gardeners

(Partially adapted from the U.S. Department of Agriculture's
1977 YEARBOOK OF AGRICULTURE*)*

ANNUAL. A plant living one year or less. During this time the plant grows, flowers, produces seed, and dies. Examples: beans, peas, sweet corn.

AXIL (leaf). The angle or upper side where the leaf is attached to the stem.

BIENNIAL. A plant that grows vegetatively during the first year and fruits and dies during the second.

BOLTING. Production of flowers and seeds by such plants as spinach, lettuce, and radishes, generally occurring when days are long and temperatures warm.

BRASSICA. A member of the mustard family. Examples include radishes, cabbage, cauliflower, broccoli, and turnips.

CLONE. A group of plants derived from an individual plant by vegetative propagation such as grafting, cutting, or divisions rather than from seed.

CLOVE. One of a group of small bulbs produced by garlic and shallot plants.

COLD FRAME. An enclosed, unheated, but covered frame useful for growing and protecting young plants in cold weather. The top is covered with glass or plastic and located so it is heated by sunlight.

COMPOST. Decayed vegetable matter such as leaves, grass clippings, or barnyard manure. It usually is mixed with soil and fertilizer. Valuable as a mulch in a garden or for improving soil texture, and in potting soils.

COOL CROPS. Vegetables that do not thrive in summer heat, such as cabbage, English peas, lettuce, or spinach.

COTYLEDON(S). Seed leaf or leaves containing stored food for initial seedling growth.

CROWN (plant). Growing point above the root where the tops or shoots develop as with lettuce, spinach, carrots, celery, and rhubarb.

CUCURBIT. A member of the gourd family, to which cucumber, muskmelon, watermelon, pumpkin, and squash belong.

CULTIVAR. A term that means "cultivated variety."A specific horticultural selection, originating and persisting under cultivation.

CURE. To prepare vegetables for storing by drying the skins. Dry onions and sweet potatoes are typical examples.

CUTTING. A segment of plant stem including a leaf node that is cut or snapped off and used to propagate a new plant.

DAMPING-OFF. A fungal disease that causes seedlings to die soon after germination, either before or after emerging from the soil.

DETERMINATE TOMATO. Stem growth stops when the terminal bud becomes a flower bud. Tomato plants of this type are also known as *self-topping* or *self-pruning*.

DIOECIOUS. A term describing plants that have exclusively male flowers on some individuals and exclusively female flowers on others. (*See* Monoecious).

DIPLOID. Having the "normal" two basic sets of chromosomes.

DIVISION. Propagation of plants by cutting them into sections, as is done with plant crowns, rhizomes, stem tubers, and tuberous roots. Each section must have at least one head or stem.

DOMINANT. Refers, loosely, to a characteristic, or, more precisely, to the underlying gene that determines that characteristic. For instance, if a plant carries genes for both red and white flower color but produces only red flowers, the gene for red is said to be dominant over the gene for white (which is termed *recessive*). (*See* Recessive).

F_1. The first filial generation, or the offspring of a given set of parents.

F_2. The second filial generation, or the offspring of the F_1's produced either by cross-fertilization among themselves or by self-fertilization.

FERTILIZATION. (1) The union of pollen with the ovule to produce seeds. This is essential in the production of edible flower parts such as tomatoes, squash, corn, strawberries, and many other garden plants. (2) The application to the soil of needed plant nutrients, such as nitrogen, phosphorous, and potash.

FLAT. A shallow wooden or plastic box, in which vegetable seeds may be sown or cuttings rooted.

FRUIT. Strictly, the ripened ovary (and its contents) of a seed plant. Loosely, the entire structure containing ripe seeds, which may include more than the ovarian tissue. A tomato is a fruit, as is the pod of a pea, the capsule of a poppy, and the "seed" of a sunflower.

FUNGICIDE. A pesticide chemical used to control plant diseases caused by fungi such as molds and mildew. (*See also* Pesticide).

GERMINATION. The sprouting of a seed and beginning of plant growth.

GREENS. Vegetables grown and harvested for their edible foliage, such as spinach, kale, collards, and turnip greens.

GROWING MEDIUM. A soil or soil substitute prepared by combining such materials as peat, vermiculite, sand, or weathered sawdust. Used for growing potted plants or germinating seed.

GROWING SEASON. The period between the last killing frost in the spring and the first killing frost in the fall.

HARDENING-OFF. Adapting plants to outdoor conditions by withholding water, lowering the temperature, or gradually eliminating the protection of a cold frame, hot bed, or greenhouse. This process conditions plants for survival when transplanted outdoors.

HARDY PLANTS. Plants adapted to winter temperatures or other climatic conditions of an area. The term *half-hardy* indicates that a plant may be able to survive in local conditions with a certain amount of protection.

HERBACEOUS PLANT. A plant that dies back to the ground in winter, such as asparagus and rhubarb.

HILL. Raising the soil in a slight mound for planting, or setting plants some distance apart.

HOST PLANT. A plant on which an insect or a disease-causing organism lives.

HOTBED. Same type of structure as a cold frame, but heated, as with an electric cable.

HUMUS. Decomposed organic material that improves the texture and productive qualities of garden soils.

HYBRID F$_1$. Plants of a first generation hybrid of two dissimilar parents. Hybrid vigor, insect or disease resistance, and uniformity are qualities of this generation. Seed from hybrid vegetables grown in your garden should not be saved for future planting. Their vigor and productive qualities generally occur only in the original hybrid seed.

IMMUNE. Free from disease infection because of resistance. Not subject to attack by a specified pest. Immunity is absolute.

IMPERFECT FLOWER. A flower containing in itself either male or female reproductive organs, but not both. (*See* Perfect Flower).

INDETERMINATE TOMATO. Terminal bud is always vegetative, and thus the stem grows indefinitely. Indeterminant plants can be trained on a trellis, a stake, or in wire cages. (*See also* Determinate Tomato.)

INFLORESCENCE. The entire floral structure of a plant.

INTERNODE. A region on a plant system between the nodes.

INTERPLANTING. The process of planting early-maturing vegetables between rows of slow-maturing vegetables to obtain maximum productivity from a garden. An example is radishes or onions planted between rows of sweet corn.

LEGGY. Weak-stemmed and spindly plants with sparse foliage caused by too much heat, shade, crowding, or overfertilization.

LEGUME. A plant that takes nitrogen from the air with the nitrifying bacteria that live on its roots. Examples are garden peas and beans.

LIFTING. Digging a plant for replanting or winter storage.

MICROCLIMATE. The climate of a small area or locality as compared to that of a country or state. For example, the climate adjacent to the north side of a home, or the influence of a lake on a portion of a county.

MILDEW. A plant disease caused by several types of fungi, recognized by the white cottony coating on affected plants.

MIST. Applying vaporized water to cuttings in the propagating stage.

MONOECIOUS. A term describing plants that have both male and female reproductive organs in different flowers on the same plant, such as cucumbers and squash. (*See* Dioecious).

NITROGEN FIXATION. The transformation of nitrogen from the air into nitrogen compounds by nitrifying bacteria on the roots of legumes.

NODE. The region of a plant stem that normally produces leaves and buds.

PARTHENOGENIC. Fruit produced without fertilization of the ovule(s). Usually seedless. (*See* Fertilization, definition 1.)

PATENTED. Plant varieties protected by a government patent, which grants exclusive rights to the patent holder.

PERENNIAL. Any plant which normally lives more than two years. Examples are artichoke, asparagus, raspberry, and rhubarb.

PERFECT FLOWER. A flower containing in itself both male and female reproductive organs. (*See* Imperfect Flower).

PESTICIDE. General term for any chemical used to control pests.

PHOTOPERIOD. Length of the light period in a day.

PHOTOPERIODISM. The effect of differences in the length of the light period upon plant growth and development.

PLANT VARIETY PROTECTED. Plant varieties protected by the U.S. Government Plant Variety Protection Act, which grants certain rights to the holder.

POLLEN. Reproductive material, usually dustlike, produced by the male part of a flower.

POLLINATION, OPEN. The transfer of pollen by natural means from the flower of one plant to another flower of the same or different plant species.

POLLINATION, SELF. The transfer of pollen from the male part of one flower to the female part of the same flower, or to another flower on the same plant.

PROPAGATION. Increasing the number of plants by planting seed or by vegetative means from cuttings, division, grafting, or layering.

RECESSIVE. Said of a gene (or of a specific plant trait or characteristic controlled by that gene) that can be masked by the corresponding dominant gene. (*See* Dominant).

RESISTANCE. The ability of a plant to restrict disease or insect damage or to withstand severe climatic conditions.

RHIZOME. A horizontal underground stem, distinguished from a root by the presence of nodes and internodes, as well as buds and scalelike leaves.

ROGUE. An off-type or diseased plant. Also, to remove such plants from the garden.

ROOT CROPS. Vegetables grown for their edible roots, such as beets, carrots, radishes, and turnips.

RUNNER. A slender, elongated, and prostrate branch that has buds and can form roots at the nodes or at the tip.

SEEDBED. Garden soil after it has been prepared for planting seeds or transplants by plowing and disking, rototilling, spading, or raking.

SEED LEAVES. *See* Cotyledon.

SEEDLING. A young plant developing from a germinating seed. It usually has the first true leaves developed.

SETS. Small onion bulbs used for early planting.

SHORT-SEASON VEGETABLES. Vegetables ready for harvest after one to two months following planting.

STAKING. Tying plants such as tomatoes to a stake to provide support.

STOLON. A slender, prostrate stem. It may produce a tuber such as a potato.

SUSCEPTIBLE. A term used to describe a plant that is unable to restrict activities of a specified pest, or to withstand an adverse environmental condition.

TENDRIL. A slender twining organ found along the stems of some plants such as grapes, which helps the vine to both climb and cling to a support.

TETRAPLOID. Having four basic sets of chromosomes.

TOLERANT. A term used to describe a plant that can endure a specified pest or an adverse environmental condition, growing and producing despite the disorder.

TRANSPLANTING. Digging up a plant and removing it from one location to another.

TRIPLOID. Having three basic sets of chromosomes.

TRUE LEAF. An ordinary leaf (as opposed to a seed leaf or *cotyledon*), which functions in the production of food by a plant.

TUBER (STEM). A thickened or swollen underground branch or stolon with numerous buds or eyes. Thickening occurs because of the accumulation of reserved food. Examples: potato, Jerusalem artichoke.

TUBEROUS ROOTS. Thickened roots, differing from stem tubers in that they lack nodes and internodes, and buds are present only at the crown or stem end. Example: Sweet potato.

VARIETIES. Closely related plants forming subdivisions of a species and having similar characteristics. (*See* Cultivar).

VEGETATIVE GROWTH. The growth of stems and foliage on plants, as opposed to flower and fruit development.

VEGETATIVE PROPAGATION. Increasing the number of plants by such methods as cuttings, grafting, or layering.

VIABLE. Alive, such as seed capable of germinating.

AVERAGE FROST DATE MAPS

Average Dates of Last Spring Frost

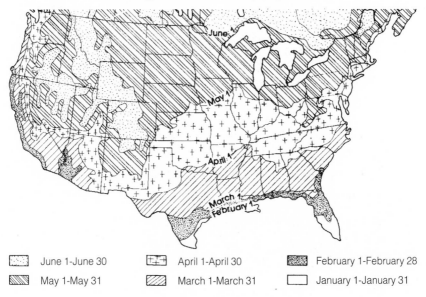

June 1-June 30	April 1-April 30	February 1-February 28
May 1-May 31	March 1-March 31	January 1-January 31

Average Dates of First Fall Frost

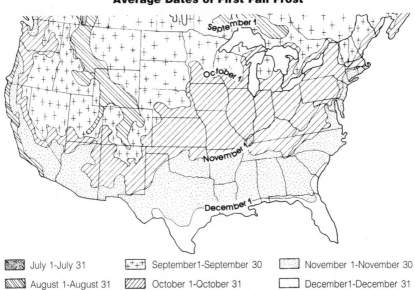

July 1-July 31	September1-September 30	November 1-November 30
August 1-August 31	October 1-October 31	December1-December 31